# BEGINNERS KETO DIET RECIPES COOKBOOK

Keto Meal Plan for Weight Loss in 3 Months

KIMBERLY M. THANE

## DISCLAIMER/LEGAL NOTICE

All rights reserved. This book may not be reproduced, transmitted by any means without the explicit permission of the copyright owner.

# TABLE OF CONTENT

DISCLAIMER/LEGAL NOTICE ........................................................................... 2

TABLE OF CONTENT ...................................................................................... 3

INTRODUCTION ............................................................................................. 8

NUTRITION .................................................................................................... 9

BENEFITS OF PRESSURE COOKING ............................................................. 10

WHAT SHOULD BE PRESSURE-COOKED? .................................................... 10

THE PRESSURE COOKER AND KETOGENIC DIET ......................................... 10

A COMPARISON OF ELECTRIC PRESSURE COOKERS .................................. 11

ESSENTIAL ACCESSORIES ........................................................................... 12

THIS COOKBOOK'S RECIPES ....................................................................... 13

BREAKFAST ................................................................................................. 14

    SOUTHWESTERN BREAKFAST CASSEROLE ........................................... 14

    SCOTCH EGGS ......................................................................................... 15

    AVOCADO EGGS BENEDICT .................................................................... 17

    SHAKSHUKA ............................................................................................ 18

    COCONUT YOGURT ................................................................................. 20

    EGG CUPS ............................................................................................... 21

    EGG LOAF ............................................................................................... 22

    MEXICAN STYLE ZUCCHINI AND POBLANOS ......................................... 23

    GREEN BEANS WITH BACON .................................................................. 24

    PALAK PANEER ....................................................................................... 25

    CREAMY POBLANO PEPPERS AND SWEET CORN .................................. 27

    QUICK INDIAN CREAMY EGGPLANT ....................................................... 28

    BABA GHANOUSH ................................................................................... 29

    CAULIFLOWER MAC AND CHEESE .......................................................... 32

    POBLANO AND CHEESE FRITTATA ......................................................... 33

    BROCCOLI, HAM AND PEPPER FRITTATA .............................................. 34

    EGG MUFFINS ......................................................................................... 35

- OMELET WITH CHIVES ... 36
- TOMATO FRITTATA ... 37
- ALMOND BREAD ... 38

VEGETABLES AND SIDES ... 40
- EASY PESTO SPAGHETTI SQUASH ... 41
- SWEET AND SOUR CABBAGE ... 42
- ASPARAGUS WITH PARMESAN ... 43
- COLLARD GREENS ... 44
- PARMESAN ARTICHOKES AND GARLIC AIOLI ... 46
- BACON BRUSSELS SPROUTS ... 47
- CAULIFLOWER PUREE ... 48
- LEMON-GARLIC BROCCOLI ... 50

SOUPS AND STEWS ... 52
- CHUNKY CLAM CHOWDER ... 53
- THREE-MEAT CHILI ... 54
- ROASTED TOMATO SOUP ... 56
- BEEF STEW ... 57
- TOM KHA GAI ... 59
- ROASTED GARLIC CAULIFLOWER SOUP ... 61
- WHITE CHICKEN CHILI ... 62
- HUNGARIAN MUSHROOM SOUP ... 64
- PUMPKIN-COCONUT SOUP ... 66
- KALE AND SAUSAGE SOUP ... 67
- NO-NOODLE CHICKEN SOUP ... 69

POULTRY, FISH, AND SHELLFISH ... 71
- LOBSTER TAIL SALAD ... 72
- MUSSELS WITH GARLIC AND WINE ... 73
- HERB AND LEMON SALMON ... 75
- SNAPPER VERACRUZ ... 76

| | |
|---|---|
| JAMBALAYA | 78 |
| SHRIMP SCAMPI | 80 |
| SIMPLE SALMON AND BROCCOLINI | 81 |
| GARLIC CHICKEN PIECES | 83 |
| CHICKEN PHO | 83 |
| SPICY TURKEY CUBES | 85 |
| HONEY TURKEY BREAST | 86 |
| PAPRIKA CHICKEN | 87 |
| KETO CHICKEN THIGH | 88 |
| CHICKEN SHAWARMA | 89 |
| CHICKEN TIKKA MASALA | 90 |
| MEXICAN STYLE CHICKEN WITH RED SALSA | 92 |
| NOW AND LATER BUTTER CHICKEN | 93 |
| DAN DAN-SYLE CHICKEN | 94 |
| SAVORY SHRIMP WITH TOMATOES AND FETA | 96 |
| EASY LOBSTER BISQUE | 97 |
| CREAMY SHRIMP SCAMPI | 98 |
| CHINESE-STYLE STEAMED GINGER SCALLION FISH | 99 |
| SESAME-GINGER CHICKEN | 101 |
| CHICKEN BRATWURST MEATBALLS WITH CABBAGE | 102 |
| HOMEMADE SLICED TURKEY AND GRAVY | 103 |
| CHICKEN KORMA | 105 |
| MOLE CHICKEN | 107 |
| BUTTER CHICKEN | 109 |
| CHICKEN CACCIATORE | 110 |
| CHICKEN BUFFALO MEATBALLS | 112 |
| BARBECUE CHICKEN WINGS | 114 |
| CREAMY ARTICHOKE CHICKEN | 115 |
| CHICKEN SHAWARMA | 117 |

- CASHEW CHICKEN ........ 118
- WHOLE CHICKEN ........ 120
- CREAMY SALSA VERDE CHICKEN ........ 122

## BEEF AND PORK ........ 124
- KIELBASA AND SAUERKRAUT ........ 125
- PORK BELLY ........ 126
- PERFECT ITALIAN MEATBALLS ........ 128
- BARBECUE PULLED PORK ........ 129
- PORK GYRO LETTUCE WRAPS WITH TZATZIKI ........ 131
- BARBACOA BEEF ........ 133
- BEEF BOURGUIGNON ........ 134
- TACO MEAT ........ 136
- FALL-OFF-THE-BONE BABY BACK RIBS ........ 138
- HAWAIIAN PORK ........ 139
- CRISPY PORK CARNITAS ........ 141
- PHILLY CHEESESTEAK ........ 142

## DESSERTS ........ 145
- MINI COCONUT-RICOTTA CUSTARD CUPS ........ 146
- LEMON CUSTARD ........ 147
- CRÈME BRULEE ........ 148
- KEY LIME PIE ........ 150
- MARBLED PUMPKIN CHEESECAKE ........ 152
- CHOCOLATE MOUSSE ........ 154
- CHEESECAKE ........ 155

## BASICS ........ 157
- BONE BROTH ........ 157
- SIMPLE SHREDDED CHICKEN ........ 159
- ZUCCHINI NOODLES ........ 160
- GUACAMOLE ........ 160

SUGAR-FREE BARBECUE SAUCE ............................................................................. 161

AVOCADO RANCH DRESSING ................................................................................ 163

GHEE ..................................................................................................................... 164

DAIRY-FREE SOUR CREAM .................................................................................... 165

# 3 MONTHS WEIGHT LOSS PLAN ............................................................................ 166

WEEK 1 .................................................................................................................. 166

WEEK 2 .................................................................................................................. 166

WEEK 3 .................................................................................................................. 166

WEEK 4 .................................................................................................................. 167

WEEK 5 .................................................................................................................. 167

WEEK 6 .................................................................................................................. 167

WEEK 7 .................................................................................................................. 168

WEEK 8 .................................................................................................................. 168

WEEK 9 .................................................................................................................. 169

WEEK 10 ................................................................................................................ 169

WEEK 11 ................................................................................................................ 169

WEEK 12 ................................................................................................................ 170

# INTRODUCTION

One of the most important things to know when going on a ketogenic diet I that you will have to adopt a diet that is high in fat, moderate in protein, and low in carbs in order to achieve ketosis. Ketosis is a fat-burning metabolic state that will help the body perform optimally. This state will encourage your body to burn fat instead of sugar. In a typical keto diet, grains, refined vegetable oils, and sugars will be replaced with quality-sourced fish and meats, healthy fat sources, and nutrient-dense vegetables. Typically, the macronutrient breakdown is 65-75% fat, 15-30% protein, and 5-10% carbohydrates. In a keto diet, the liver will help convert fatty acids into ketone bodies for the body to use as its primary source of fuel, instead of going through the process of breaking carbohydrates down to glucose for fuel.

Some of the benefits of sticking to a keto diet are improved composition of the body, improved skin, better digestion, and sustainable energy. For someone like me who is passionate about cooking, going ketogenic gives me an opportunity to experiment and enjoy low-carb meals.

The pressure cooker has been beneficial in preparing these meals as cooking has become faster, more flavored, and enjoyable.

The recipes provided in this book will help you cook confidently with any version of the pressure cooker you have.

# NUTRITION

Every individual requires a nutrition strategy that matches his or her genetic makeup, goals, and level of activity. What works for one person may not necessarily work for the other, which is why it is important to know what works best for you.

Going keto is a very good way to eat. The following tips will help you achieve success:

- Go for Quality Food: The quality of the food you eat is just as important as eating the right type of food. The nutritional value of your food depends on the way the produce you eat is grown and processed, as well as the way the animals you eat are raised. Quality food is gotten from organic, pasture-raised, grass-fed, wild-caught, and locally-raised options.
- Eat Real Food: Not all keto meals are healthy and nutrient-dense. As a matter of fact, you may be in a state of ketosis but still be unhealthy due to the consumption of processed foods, processed meat, and processed cheese. Let your choice of food come from healthy and nutrient-dense sources, instead of a bag or box.
- Eat the Right Kind of Fat: The primary source of fuel in a ketogenic diet could be either dietary fat or body fat. Processed and refined vegetable oils and seed oils found in most of the store-bought dressings, processed foods, and condiments should be avoided. These unhealthy fat sources are the major causes of unwanted inflammatory and metabolic conditions. Healthy fats and oils like coconut oil, butter, ghee, avocado oil, and olive oil should replace sunflower oil, margarine, soybean oil, and canola oil. The importance of the quality and source of your food cannot be overemphasized.
- Enjoy the Journey: The ketogenic lifestyle is quite easy to maintain and gives meals that taste delicious and are satisfying. You can adopt this eating style, enjoy it, and still have flexibility within this lifestyle. When on a keto diet, your focus should be on progress, not perfection and you should go gentle on yourself. Do not make food your enemy; instead food should help you optimize your health and achieve your goals. Indulging in a doughnut that is jelly-filled and covered with powdered sugar once in a while is totally okay. Just take it one step at a time

# BENEFITS OF PRESSURE COOKING

The pressure cooker is an amazing kitchen appliance for preparing meals that are flavorful, high in fat, and low in carb. The Instant Pot makes cooking delightful and eliminates the need for using a stove or oven. Here are some of the benefits of using pressure cookers:

- Cooks Fast: Pressure cookers cook food fast compared to stove tops or ovens. In most cases, food cooks 25 to 30% faster when done with a pressure cooker.
- Better Results: The results gotten from cooking with a pressure cooker are usually better and more consistent than conventional cooking methods. It is even easier to peel hard-boiled eggs when they are cooked using a pressure cooker.
- Multi-purpose: With a pressure cooker, it is easier to cook one-pot meals easily and efficiently, especially because of the Sauté or Browning function that pressure cookers have.
- Saves Energy: Pressure cookers cook faster than conventional cooking methods and also use far less water while cooking. This makes them the most energy-efficient cooking appliances.
- Saves Flavor and Nutrients: Nutrients and flavor get lost when food is exposed to heat for extended periods. The reduced cooking time also helps save water, and reduces the number of minerals and nutrients that dissolve while cooking. Therefore, cooking with a pressure cooker makes your food more nutrient-dense and well-flavored.

## WHAT SHOULD BE PRESSURE-COOKED?

The pressure cooker is great for cooking meals that would traditionally take a long time to cook. Pressure cookers typically cook food with steam and high heat. Some of the foods the pressure cooker cooks quickly and excellently are soups, stocks, dried beans, legumes, braises, stews, hard vegetables, sauces, and grains.

## THE PRESSURE COOKER AND KETOGENIC DIET

Keto and pressure cooking go very well together. The pressure cooker can quickly cook your nutrient-rich vegetables, quality-sourced meats, and fat-filled stews, condiments, and sauces. It does this very efficiently with minimal loss of nutrients and flavors.

# A COMPARISON OF ELECTRIC PRESSURE COOKERS

Although at their core, pressure cookers cook the same way, there are some differences that are worthy of note.

**Instant Pot:** These multi-cookers come in 3 sizes, which are: 3-quart, 6-quart, and 8-quart. The Instant Pot comes with many preprogrammed settings and slow-cooks settings too. Its inner pot is made of stainless steel and it comes with a ceramic nonstick pot which is available separately. They also come in different models, but the pressure level of the Lux model is adjustable and has a yogurt setting. The customer service is excellent and it has many accessories available. On the downside, the reprogrammed settings of the Instant Pot are not always accurate. More so, the different models have different preset times, which makes it hard to follow same recipes for all models of the Instant Pot.

**Breville Fast Slow Pro:** This multi-cooker is only available in 6-quart size. It functions mainly as a slow cooker but has many preprogrammed settings for slow cooking and pressure cooking. The inner pot of this pressure cooker is made of nonstick ceramic and its pressure level is adjustable. You can even select the release method at the start of the cooking cycle. The pressure release button is also rightly placed on the front so your hand is quite far from the steam when you are releasing pressure. However, the lid of this cooker is attached to the base and it has an arm that cannot be detached which makes it harder to store.

**Power Pressure Cooker XL:** Available in three sizes, which are: 6-quart, 8-quart, and 10-quart, this multi-cooker has adjustable pressure levels, nonstick inner pot, pre-programmed settings, and slow-cook settings. It is also one of the few electric cookers with a 10-quart model. However, its nonstick inner pot is not quite durable.

# ESSENTIAL ACCESSORIES

Having some necessary accessories will help bring out the best in you and your pressure cooker. Below is a list of some of the best accessories and their uses.

- Extra Sealing Ring: This ring helps absorb the flavors of different foods. The use of separate sealing rings for sweet and savory dishes will prevent your food from having a different taste.
- Glass Lid: This accessory is important when your pressure cooker is performing other functions apart from pressure cooking. This glass lid will prevent your food from splattering outside the pot while you are using the Sauté setting. More so, with the glass lid, you can store the entire inner pot in the refrigerator.
- Ramekins/Custard Jars/Mason Jars: These are necessary when making single-serving egg dishes or desserts.
- Steamer Basket: This accessory is perfect for steaming vegetables, and will prevent them from falling through the basket and getting mush in the water.
- Silicone Cups: Although these can be used like the ramekins, custard jars, and mason jars, they have flexible surfaces that makes it easier to remove cooked food. Silicone cups are great for cooking eggs Benedict.
- 7-Inch Spring-form Pan: This popular accessory fit perfectly into the pressure cooker and allows you to easily make quiches and cheesecakes.

## THIS COOKBOOK'S RECIPES

Contained in this cookbook are some of my favorite recipes for pressure cooker, and some staples and basics which do not require pressuring cooking. Time for preparation, cook time under pressure, method of pressure release, and total time for cooking are all specified in this cookbook. Also included are dietary labels and nutrition information in grams and macronutrients in percentages. You will also find tips in some of the recipes for substitution options, ingredients used, and cooking techniques.

# BREAKFAST

## SOUTHWESTERN BREAKFAST CASSEROLE

This casserole is great for every meal.

Serves: 6

Time for Preparation: 10 minutes

Time for Pressure Cooking: 12 minutes on high pressure

Time for Release: 10 minutes Natural, then Quick

Total Time: 40 minutes

Gluten-free and Nut-free

**Ingredients:**

½ cup of heavy cream

½ cup of half-and-half

½ teaspoon of sea salt

¼ teaspoon of freshly ground black pepper

1 tablespoon of Ghee

1 pound of crumbled and divided cooked Mexican chorizo

2 (4-ounce) of cans whole green chiles, drained and blotted dry

4 big eggs

4 ounces of Monterey Jack or some other grated mild cheese (about 2½) cups), divided

**Procedure**

- Whisk the eggs very well inside a medium bowl. Add the half-and-half, cream, pepper, and salt then whisk together to combine.
- Get a 1½-quart baking dish then use the ghee to coat the sides and bottom. Cut open the chiles and put them in the bottom of the dish so

that it forms a single layer. Sprinkle 1/3 of the cheese on the chiles and top it with half of the chorizo. Use another layer of chiles to top this along with 1/3 of the cheese. Top this with the remaining chorizo and add another layer of chiles if you have any left.

- Pour the egg mixture on the casserole until at least ½-inch of the dish is filled from the top. Use aluminum foil to cover the dish without crimping it down to avoid expansion of the casserole.
- Get a pressure cooker and pour 1½ cups of water into it. Place a trivet with handles inside the cooker and keep the casserole on it. Use a foil sling if your trivet does not have handles.
- Lock the lid securely and set on High Pressure. The time should be set to 12 minutes and then released naturally for 10 minutes after cooking. Quick release whatever pressure is left before unlocking and removing the lid.
- Take the casserole out of the pot. Put a knife in the center to test the casserole. If the knife comes out clean, it meant it is done; but if it isn't clean, you should put the casserole back into the pressure cooker, lock the lid and allow to cook for another 5 minutes.
- While cooking the casserole, the oven should be preheated to broil. Get rid of the foil and sprinkle the cheese set aside on top of the casserole. The dish should be placed under the broiler until the cheese melts and is browned, which should take about 4 minutes.
- Allow the casserole to cool for some minutes before you serve.

**Per Serving Contains**: 582 Calories, 4g Total Carbs, 50g Total Fat, 27g Protein, 4g Net Carbs, 1g Sugar, 0g Fiber.

**Macros:** 19% Protein, 78% Fat, and 3% Carbs.

## SCOTCH EGGS

**Serves: 4**

**Time for Preparation: 10 minutes**

**Sauté: 15 minutes**

**Time for Pressure Cooking: 3 minutes on High Pressure**

**Time for Release: Quick**

**Total Time:** 40 minutes

**Gluten-free, Dairy-free, and Nut-free**

**Ingredients:**

¼ cup of avocado oil

¾ pound of bulk breakfast sausage

4 large eggs

**Preparation:**

- Get your pressure cooker and pour 1¾ cups of water into it then put the trivet in it. Place your eggs very gently on the trivet.
- Get an ice bath ready by half-filling a medium bowl with cold water and adding a few ice cubes to it.
- Place the lid over the pressure cooker and lock securely. The steam release knob should be sealed. Set to High pressure and set time to 3 minutes. Then quick release the pressure after cooking. Unlock the lid and remove it.
- Use tongs to move the eggs to the ice bath and allow it cool for about 4 minutes. When the eggs are cool enough to handle, peel them and blot them till they are dry.
- Split the sausage into 4 then make each of the pieces flattened into an oval shape. Place one egg each on an oval sausage then wrap the egg carefully with the sausage until the edges are sealed.
- Pour out the water from the pressure cooker pot then dry it. Choose either Browning or Sauté, then set to medium heat. Pour the avocado oil into the cooker and heat until it shimmers. Put in the eggs wrapped in sausage and let them cook for 1 – 2 minutes. Ensure all sides of the sausages are browned then remove one from the pot and test using a tip of the knife just to make sure it is properly cooked. Return to the pot if not properly cooked and allow to cook till it is done.
- Get the eggs out and place them on a rack then allow to cool for some minutes. Serve.

**Per Serving Contains:** 482 Calories, 2g Total Carbs, 44g Total Fat, 17g Protein, 2g Net Carbs, 1g Sugar, 0g Fiber.

**Macros:** 14% Protein, 84% Fat, and 2% Carbs.

# AVOCADO EGGS BENEDICT

**Serves:** 4

**Time for Preparation:** 5 minutes

**Time for Steaming:** 3 minutes on High Pressure

**Time for Release:** 3 minutes Natural, then Quick

**Total Time:** 15 minutes

**Gluten-free and Nut-free**

**Ingredients:**

¼ teaspoon of paprika

¼ teaspoon of cayenne pepper

¼ teaspoon of sea salt, add for more seasoning

1 tablespoon of avocado oil

1 tablespoon of freshly squeezed lemon juice

2 pitted, peeled, and sliced avocados

4 slices of cooked uncured bacon

4 large eggs with 2 large egg yolks

4 tablespoons of melted, unsalted grass-fed butter

Freshly ground black pepper

**Preparation:**

- Use avocado oil to grease 4 silicone cups then crack a whole egg into each prepared silicone cup.
- Get a pressure cooker and pour 1 cup of water into it then place a trivet inside. Place the egg cups very gently on the trivet. Lock the lid properly and seal then set the steam on High for 2 to 3 minutes.

- Mix the egg yolks, paprika, cayenne, salt, and lemon juice into a blender and blend for 5 – 10 seconds until they mix properly.
- Adjust the blender to high speed and pour out the hot melted butter in a thin stream so the mixture will quickly get thick. Get a pan of hot tap water and place the blender jar inside it so the hollandaise sauce will remain warm till it is time to serve.
- After cooking, naturally release the pressure for 3 minutes then quick release any pressure remaining. Get the silicone cups out of the cooker carefully.
- Split the slices of avocado into 4 plates and top it with poached eggs and cooked bacon. Pour the hollandaise sauce on top then use pepper and salt to season it.

**Tip:** Cook the eggs for 2 to 3 minutes to get well-poached eggs.

**Per Serving Contains**: 393 Calories, 8g Total Carbs, 35g Total Fat, 13g Protein, 3g Net Carbs, 2g Sugar, 5g Fiber.

**Macros:** 13% Protein, 79% Fat, and 8% Carbs.

## SHAKSHUKA

This North African and Arab staple cuisine is made using eggs that are cooked in spiced tomato sauce with fresh crumbled feta and hummus toppings.

**Serves: 4**

**Time for Preparation: 3 minutes**

**Sauté: 8 minutes**

**Time for Pressure Cooking: 0 minutes on Low Pressure**

**Time for Release: Quick**

**Total Time: 22 minutes**

**Gluten-free and Nut-free**

**Ingredients:**

½ diced medium zucchini

¼ cup of chopped fresh cilantro

¼ cup of chicken broth or bone broth

1 diced onion

1 teaspoon of paprika

1 teaspoon of chili powder

1 teaspoon of ground cumin

2 (14.5-ounce) cans of diced tomatoes and juices

3 tablespoons of avocado oil

4 minced garlic cloves

4 tablespoons of hummus

5 ounces of crumbled feta cheese

6 large eggs

**Preparation:**

1. Select Sauté or Browning on the pressure cooker then set on medium heat. Put the avocado oil in the cooker and heat it until it shimmers. Add the garlic and onion to the cooker and allow to Sauté or 3 to 5 minutes, until it becomes translucent and fragrant. Add chili powder, cumin, zucchini, and paprika to the pot. Allow to Sauté for another minute or 2.
2. Turn the pressure cooker off and add the diced tomatoes with their juices, along with the bone broth. Stir until properly mixed then crack the eggs carefully into the tomato mixture, evenly spaced so as not to break the yolks.
3. Lock the lid securely into place and seal it. Adjust pressure to Low and time to 0 minutes. (You can set it to 1 minute if you cannot set to 0 minutes, but be sure to release the pressure when the pot starts counting down.) Quick release the pressure after cooking. Unlock the lid and remove it.
4. Use a ladle to spoon off the liquid that has gathered on the eggs. Allow cooling a little before topping with the crumbled feta cheese, hummus, and the cilantro.

**Per Serving Contains:** 378 Calories, 15g Total Carbs, 26g Total Fat, 18g Protein, 12g Net Carbs, 8g Sugar, 3g Fiber.

**Macros:** 20% Protein, 64% Fat, and 16% Carbs

## COCONUT YOGURT

**Serves:** 4

**Time for Preparation:** 2 minutes

**Cook:** About 30 minutes

**Incubation:** 10 to 12 hours

**Total Time:** 12 hours and 32 minutes, with an additional 4 to 6 hours to chill

**Gluten-free, Dairy-free, and Nut-free**

**Ingredients:**

1 teaspoon of vanilla extract

2 (13.5-ounce) cans of full-fat coconut cream

2-3 teaspoons of grass-fed gelatin

4 probiotic capsules of high quality

Stevia (optional)

**Preparation:**

- Place the coconut cream in the pressure cooker then lock the lid into place. Set the steam knob to the open position then press the yogurt function button then set to Boil setting. When it is done, unlock and remove the lid.
- Get the cooker pot out of the pressure cooker then allow the coconut cream cool until it gets to 100oF to 115oF. Open the probiotic capsules then empty the contents into the coconut cream then whisk properly until it mixes properly. Get rid of the empty capsules.
- Put the pot back on the pressure cooker, then press the yogurt button and set back to normal. Adjust the time to 10 to 12 hours. The yogurt becomes tarter the longer it incubates.
- After the completion of incubation, then unlock the lid. Get the inner pot out of the pressure cooker then pour the yogurt into a food processor or blender. Mix the gelatin in a small bowl and add 3 to 4 tablespoons of cold

water. Mix it very well then allow to sit for a minute so it can bloom. Put the vanilla, gelatin mixture, and stevia (optional) into the blender. Blend until it combines properly.
- Allow the yogurt to cool then pour them into glass containers. Close tightly with a lid and store up in the refrigerator for about 4 to 6 hours. Stir the yogurt if it separates when cooled. Store it in the refrigerator for about a week.

**Per Serving Contains:** 251 Calories, 3g Total Carbs, 23g Total Fat, 8g Protein, 3g Net Carbs, 0g Sugar, 0g Fiber.

**Macros:** 13% Protein, 83% Fat, and 4% Carbs

## EGG CUPS

**Prep Time: 10 minutes**

**Cooking Time: 5 Minutes**

**Serves: 4**

**Ingredients:**

4 eggs

1 teaspoon of salt

¼ cup of half-and-half

1 teaspoon of freshly ground pepper (black)

½ cups of shredded cheese for garnish purpose

Vegetable oil or unsalted butter to grease the jars

1 cup of vegetable (diced) i.e. Onions, mushrooms, bell peppers or tomatoes

½ cup of cheddar cheese (grated)

2 tablespoons of fresh chopped cilantro

**Directions:**

- Get the butter or oil and grease the inside of each jar generously. You can use silicone brush for an even spread.
- Get a medium bowl and beat the eggs then stir in the cheese, vegetables, pepper, salt, half-and-half and cilantro. Get four heatproof half-pint wide mouth jars or any other container that is heat proof. Carefully put the lids on the jars but make sure you do not tighten. This is because the lids help keep moisture out of the eggs.)
- Get two cups of water and pour into the instant pot cooking pot. In the pot, place a trivet and then carefully place on top of the trivet, three egg jars.
- Make sure to lock the lid. On the instant pot menu, select pressure cook or manual and then tune the pressure upwards to high. Allow cooking for the next 5 minutes. Quick-release pressure after cooking is complete.
- Open the lids on the jars and then proceed to top egg with your preferred cheese.
- Go on to put the eggs in an air fryer or under the broiler for 3 minutes until the cheese on top is observed to be lightly browned.

**Nutrition:** Calorie: 239, Fat: 17g, Carbs: 5g, Fiber: 2g, Sugar: 2g, Protein: 15g

## EGG LOAF

**Prep Time: 5 minutes**

**Cooking Time: 4 minutes**

**Servings: 6**

**Ingredients:**

Butter (unsalted) for greasing the bowl

6 eggs

2 cups of water (for steaming)

**Directions:**

- Apply a generous amount of butter on the heatproof bowl for greasing.

- Crack the eggs leaving the yolk intact and use aluminum foil to cover the bowl then set aside.
- To the instant pot, pour water into it and then place trivet on top.
- Then place on the trivet, the foil-covered bowl with eggs in it.
- Close the lid and select pressure cook, set to high pressure. You allow cooking for 4 minutes and them quick release pressure.
- As carefully as possible, take out the bowl from the pot. Pop the egg loaf out from the bowl. You should see a loaf of egg white and only few egg yolk spots.
- Cut the egg loaf to taste either coarse or fine. You are free to mix a little mayonnaise for egg salad, turn it with little salt, pepper and butter for a quick meal.

**Nutrition:** Calories: 74, Total Fat: 5g, Net Carbs: 0g, Total Carbs: 0g, Fiber: 0g, Sugar: 0G, Protein: 6g

## MEXICAN STYLE ZUCCHINI AND POBLANOS

**Prep Time: 5 minutes**

**Cooking Time: 2 Minutes**

**Serves: 6**

**Ingredients:**

1 tablespoon of vegetable oil

2 teaspoons of unsalted butter

2 poblano peppers (cut lengthwise ½ inch strips and seeded)

½ thinly sliced onion

1 pound of crushed pork

1 tablespoon of shredded garlic

1 zucchini sliced into thick rounds

½ cup of chicken broth

1 crookneck squash (yellow) sliced into thick rounds

1 teaspoon of salt

½ teaspoon cumin (ground)

1 tablespoon sour cream or Mexican crema

**Directions:**

- Select Sauté on the instant pot and set to high heat to preheat. Pour in oil when the inner pot is hot until the oil is seen to be shimmering. In a single layer, add the poblano strips in batches if you desire and char both sides. Occasionally flip for about 10 minutes.
- To the pot, add the butter and allow melting. After it has melted, add garlic, onion and sauté until soft. This should take 2 minutes.
- Break the ground pork in chunks and add making sure to mix properly with the vegetables. Make sure to cook and look for when the lumps break up in the meat and also cooked half-way, this should take 4-5 minutes.
- Add the squash, broth, salt, cumin and zucchini to the pot.
- Lock the lid and select pressure cook or manual then set to low pressure. Allow for 2 minutes to cook. After cooking is complete, quick release pressure and unlock the lid.
- Stir the crema so it mixes into the sauce.

**Nutrition**: Calories: 24, Total Carbs: 3g, Net Carbs: 2g, Fiber: 1g, Total Fat: 20g, Sugar: 1g, Protein: 14g

## GREEN BEANS WITH BACON

**Prep Time: 10 minutes**

**Cook Time: 4 minutes**

**Servings: 6**

**Ingredients:**

Diced bacon, 6 slices

Diced onion, 1 cup

Halved green beans, 4 cups

¼ cup of water

Salt, 1 teaspoon

Ground black pepper, 1 teaspoon

**Directions:**

- Select sauté on the instant pot and adjust to high heat for preheating. Pour in the onion and bacon and then sauté for 2 - 3 minutes.
- To the pot, add pepper, water, green beans and salt
- Close the lid and select pressure cook or manual and set pressure to high. Allow to cook for 4 minutes and then quick-release the pressure. You can proceed to unlock the lid.
- If after tasting, you choose to add a little more pepper and salt before serving, its fine.

**Nutrition**: Calories: 165, Total Carbs: 6g, Net carbs: 3g, Fiber: 3g, Total fat: 13g, Sugar: 2g, Protein: 6g

## PALAK PANEER

**Prep time: 10 minutes**

**Cooking time: 4 minutes**

**Servings: 6**

**Ingredients:**

2 teaspoons of vegetable oil

5 cloves of chopped garlic

1 tablespoon of fresh ginger (chopped)

½ jalapeno or Serrano chile (chopped)

1 onion (large, yellow, chopped)

1 pound of spinach (fresh)

2 chopped tomatoes

2 teaspoons of cumin (ground)

½ teaspoon of cayenne

2 teaspoons of Garam Masala

1 teaspoon of turmeric (ground)

1 teaspoon of salt

½ cup of water

1 ½ cups of paneer cubes

½ cup of cream (heavy whipping cream)

**Directions:**

- Select sauté and adjust to high heat to preheat pot. Allow for the inner pot to become hot and then proceed to pour oil in. allow shimmering. Add ginger, garlic and chile. Sauté for 2-3 minutes.
- Add the spinach, tomato, onion, cayenne, cumin, turmeric, garam masala, water and salt.
- Close the lid and select pressure cook or manual. Make sure to set pressure to high and allow cooking for4 minutes. Allow pressure to release naturally for 5 minutes and then proceed to quick release the remaining pressure. You can now open the lid.
- Tilting slightly the pot, puree the mixture with an immersion blender. You can make the mixture puree till very smooth or slightly chunky depending on your preference.

- Stir gently the paneer and use a drizzle of cream to top each serving.

**Nutrition:** Calories: 185, Total Carbs: 9g, Net carbs: 7g, Fiber: 2g, Total fat: 14g, Sugar: 2g, Protein: 7g

## CREAMY POBLANO PEPPERS AND SWEET CORN

**Prep time: 10 minutes**

**Cooking time: 1 minute**

**Servings: 6**

**Ingredients:**

1 tablespoon of vegetable oil

2 poblano peppers cut into ½ inch thick in strips

¾ thinly sliced red onion

½ cup of frozen corn

¼ cup of water

1-2 teaspoons of salt

1 teaspoon of cumin (grounded)

½ cup of heavy cream (whipping)

½ lemon juice

2 tablespoons of sour cream

**Directions:**

- Select sauté on instant pot and set to high heat to preheat pot. Pour oil into preheated pot and allow until it shimmers. Proceed to add in the skin-side of poblano in a single layer and allow char a bit undisturbed for 5-8 minutes.
- Add the corn, cumin, water, salt and onion to the pot.

- Close the lid and select pressure cook or manual setting pressure to low. Cook for 1 minute and quick release pressure. You can then unlock the lid.
- In a separate bowl while vegetable cooks, mix in the heavy cream, sour cream and lemon juice. This will make crema. Stir in the crema into the pot after the vegetable has finished cooking.
- To the finished vegetables, sprinkle some cumin if desired for fragrance.

**Nutrition:** Calories: 123, Total Carbs: 4g, Net carbs: 3g, Fiber: 1g, Total fat: 11g, Sugar: 1g, Protein: 2g

## QUICK INDIAN CREAMY EGGPLANT

**Prep time: 15 minutes**

**Cook time: 4 minutes**

**Servings: 6**

**Ingredients:**

½ teaspoons of peanut oil

1 small thinly sliced onion

1 chopped tomato

4 cups of eggplant (chopped)

¼ teaspoon of turmeric (ground)

¼ teaspoon of cayenne

¼ teaspoon of Garam Masala

¼ teaspoon of chaat masala or amchoor

¼ teaspoon of chana masala or Goda masala

¼ teaspoon of salt

¼ cup of heavy cream (whipping)

**Directions:**

- To the inner cooking pot, pour in the oil. Put in the tomato, onion and eggplant on top. Make sure the tomato and onion are at the bottom to create much-needed moisture for cooking because you won't be adding any more water.
- Sprinkle some turmeric, garam masala, Goda masala, cayenne and salt on the vegetables. Don't stir.
- Close the lid of the instant pot and adjust to low pressure after selecting manual. Allow for 4 minutes to cook.
- After cooking, leave pressure to naturally release for about 10 minutes and then let off the remaining pressure with quick-release.
- Select sauté and proceed to set to high heat. Allow mixture to bubble and then add cream. Make sure to stir properly to incorporate. Leave the cream for about 2 minutes to thicken and serve.

**Nutrition:** Calorie: 73, Total Carbs: 6g, Net carbs: 3g, Fiber: 3g, Total Fat: 5g, Sugar: 2g, Protein: 1g

## BABA GHANOUSH

**Prep time: 10 minutes**

**Cook time: 3 minutes**

**Serving: 1 ½**

**Ingredients:**

6 divided tablespoons of vegetable oil

1 peeled eggplant halved crosswise and into ½ inch thick length

5 cloves of minced garlic

½ teaspoon of salt

½ cup of water

2 tablespoons of tahini

1 or 2 tablespoons of lemon juice (squeezed)

¼ teaspoon of liquid smoke

2 tablespoons of parsley (chopped)

1 tablespoon of oil (olive extra-virgin)

Pinched paprika (smoked)

**Directions:**

- Select sauté and set to high heat to preheat the pot. Allow to heat and add 2 tablespoons of oil. Allow to heat until it shimmer.
- To the inner pot, add a layer of eggplant slice and allow to char. Do not disturb until properly charred. The char will bring out the desired smoky taste. The sliced char is expected to shrink a bit; you then move them to a side of the pot to allow you add more eggplant slices. Add more oil to each set of sliced eggplant added to the pot. It will take 10-15 minutes to char all eggplants. Scrape with spoon or spatula all eggplants from the pot once they are charred.
- Add water, salt and garlic to the pot containing charred eggplant slices.
- Lock the lid and select pressure cook or manual and set to high pressure and allow cooking for 3 minutes. Quick-release the pressures once cooking is complete and open the lid.
- If you notice much water at the bottom of the instant pot after opening the lid, set the instant pot to sauté to let some of its steam off.
- Using an immersion blender, slightly tilt the pot and puree the eggplant mixture roughly. You can puree until smooth if you are feeding to a baby but if not, there will be no need.
- Stir in the lemon juice, liquid smoke and tahini. You can then taste and adjust if necessary.

- Spoon it into a bowl and top it with olive oil and parsley, then sprinkle with smoked paprika.
- Serve with vegetables such as celery or green beans.

**Nutrition:** Calories: 96, Total Carbs: 3g, Net carbs: 1g, Fiber: 2g, Total Fat: 9g, Sugar: 1g, Protein: 1g

# CAULIFLOWER MAC AND CHEESE

**Prep time: 5 minutes**

**Cook time: 5 minutes**

**Serving: 4**

**Ingredients:**

2 cups of cauliflower rice

2 tablespoons of room temperature cream cheese

½ cup of half-and-half

½ cup of cheddar cheese (grated)

1 teaspoon of salt

1 teaspoon of black pepper (freshly ground)

**Directions:**

- Get a heat-resistant bowl and mix the cream cheese, cauliflower, cheddar cheese, half-and-half, pepper and salt together. Using an aluminum foil, cover the bowl.
- To the instant pot inner pot, pour in 2 cups of water and place carefully, a trivet in the pot and place on top of the trivet, the bowl.
- Close the lid and select pressure cook or manual and set pressure to high and allow cooking for 5 minutes. After cooking is complete, allow pressure naturally release for 10 minutes and quick-release to let off the remaining pressure. Open the lid and remove the lid carefully, then proceed to remove the foil.
- Take the cauliflower and place under the broiler. Within 3-5 minutes under the broiler, the cheese will become brown and bubble. Serve immediately.

**Nutrition:** Calories: 134, Total Carbs: 4g, Net carbs: 3g, Fiber: 1g, Total fat: 11g, Sugar: 2g, Protein: 6g

# POBLANO AND CHEESE FRITTATA

**Prep time: 10 minutes**

**Cook time: 20 minutes**

**Servings: 4**

**Ingredients:**

Unsalted butter or vegetable oil

4 eggs

1 cup of half-and-half

1 can of green chiles (chopped, 10-ounce)

1 ½ teaspoons of salt

½ teaspoon of cumin (ground)

1 cup of shredded cheese (Mexican blend)

¼ cup of fresh cilantro (chopped)

**Directions:**

- Get a 6 by 3-inch pan and generously grease with butter or oil.
- Get a medium bowl and beat the egg then stir in the chile, half-and-half, cumin, salt and ½ cup of cheese. Get an aluminum foil and use to cover the mixture after pouring into the prepared pan
- To the instant pot inner cooking pot, pour 2 cups of water and place in a trivet stand. Place the pan on top of the trivet.
- Close the lid and select pressure cook or manual and set to high pressure and allow cooking for 20 minutes. After cooking, allow pressure to naturally release for 10 minutes and then allow for the remaining pressure to release by quick-release. Open the lid.
- Remove carefully, the pan from inside the instant pot and then take off the foil. On the frittata, sprinkle the ½ remaining cup of cheese. Proceed to place under broiler and allow for 2-5 minutes or till you notice the cheese brown of bubbling.

- Allow the frittata for 5-10 minutes. Get a knife and carefully loosen the frittata from the pan by the side. When the frittata is loosened, hold a plate on top and carefully invert the frittata into the plate. You can flip it once more depending on the side you wish to face up.

**Nutrition:** Calories: 283, Total Carbs: 7g, Net carbs: 6g, Fiber: 1g, Total fat: 22g, Sugar: 1g, Protein: 16g

## BROCCOLI, HAM AND PEPPER FRITTATA

**Prep time: 10 minutes**

**Cook time: 20 minutes**

**Serving: 4**

**Ingredients:**

Unsalted butter or vegetable oil

1 cup of bell peppers (sliced)

8 ounces of cubed ham

2 cups of broccoli florets (frozen)

4 eggs

1 cup of half-and-half

1 teaspoon of salt

2 teaspoons of black pepper (ground)

1 cup of cheddar cheese (grated)

**Directions:**

- Using a silicon brush, grease the 6-by-3 pan properly to prevent egg sticking to it.

- Place the cut peppers in the pan followed by the ham (cubed) on top. Cover this with frozen broccoli
- Get a medium bowl and mix together the half-and-half, eggs, pepper and salt. Stir the cheese in.
- Pour over the ham and vegetable, the egg mixture and cover with silicon lid or aluminum foil.
- To the instant cooking pot inner pot, pour in 2 cups of water and place a trivet inside the pot. On the trivet, place the covered pan.
- Close the lid, select pressure cook or manual and set to high pressure and allow cooking for 20 minutes. After cooking, allow pressure to naturally release for 10 minutes and then quick-release the remaining pressure and open the lid.
- Gently take out the pan from the pot and take off foil. Allow the frittata for 5-10minutes. With the aid of a knife, carefully loosen the side of the frittata and flip on a plate. Depending on where you want facing up, flip again.
- It is ready to be served but you may go ahead and broil the frittata for 3-4 minutes to brown the top.

**Nutrition:** Calories: 396, Total Carbs: 9g, Net carbs: 6g, Fiber: 3g, Total fat: 27g, Sugar: 3g, Protein: 30g

## EGG MUFFINS

**Prep time: 7 minutes**

**Cooking time: 8 minutes**

**Servings: 4**

**Ingredients:**

4 eggs

½ teaspoon of olive oil

½ teaspoon of salt

¼ cup of cilantro (fresh)

**Directions:**

- Get a bowl and beat in the eggs. Whisk properly and continue until smooth.
- Get your salt and olive oil and sprinkle some on top the egg.
- To the egg mixture, cut the cilantro and stir in properly.
- Get a muffin mold and pour in the egg mixture.
- Get the instant pot bowl and pour in ½ cup of water.
- Place the trivet in the instant pot and place the muffin mold on it.
- Close the cover of the instant pot and adjust pressure mode.
- Allow cooking for up to 8 minutes.
- Allow pressure release naturally for 2 minutes and remove the muffin mold from the instant pot.
- Proceed to serve and enjoy.

**Nutrition:** Calories: 71, Fiber: 0.2g, fat: 5g, protein: 5.7g, carbs: 1g

## OMELET WITH CHIVES

**Prep time: 10 minutes**

**Cooking time: 20 minutes**

**Servings: 2**

**Ingredients:**

3 eggs

2 oz. of chives

¼ teaspoon of olive oil

1 tomato cherry

¼ teaspoon of salt

2 tablespoons of milk (coconut)

**Directions:**

- Get a bowl and beat the eggs in whisking them till smooth.
- Cut the cherry tomato and chives.
- Add the cut tomato and chive into the egg whisked earlier.
- Add salt, olive oil and coconut milk and stir well.
- To the inner pot of the instant pot, pour in 1 cup of water.
- Get your trivet and put it into the instant pot.
- Get the glass bowl containing the egg mixture and place it on top of the trivet.
- Close the pot.
- Set the pressure to high and allow cooking for 20 minutes.
- After 20 minutes, the omelet will be cooked. Quick-release pressure.
- Serve and enjoy.

**Nutrition:** Calories: 149, carbs: 3.7g, fiber: 1.4g, fat: 10.9g, protein: 9.6g

## TOMATO FRITTATA

**Prep time 7 minutes**

**Cook time: 3 minutes**

**Serves: 4**

**Ingredients:**

4 eggs

1 sliced tomato

½ teaspoon of salt

1 teaspoon of cooking fat (keto)

1 tablespoon of parsley (chopped)

½ teaspoon of paprika

**Directions:**

- Get a bowl and beat in the eggs
- After whisking, add chopped parsley, salt and paprika then stir.
- To the instant pot, pour in 1 cup of water and put in the trivet.
- Get the glass bowl and pour in the egg mixture.
- To the mixture, add the keto cooking fat and sliced tomato and gently stir with the aid of a fork.
- Close the lid and set to high for 3 minutes.
- Quick-release and turn meal to serving plate.

**Nutrition**: calories: 67, carbs: 1.1g, fiber: 0.3g, fat: 4.4g, protein: 5.8g

## ALMOND BREAD

**Prep time: 15 minutes**

**Cook time: 60 minutes**

**Servings: 6**

**Ingredients:**

4 oz. of almond flour

1 egg

1 banana

1/3 teaspoon of baking powder

½ teaspoon of vanilla extract

¼ teaspoon of stevia liquid

14 teaspoons of sea salt

½ teaspoon of olive oil

**Directions:**

- Chop the peeled banana and mash
- Beat the egg and mix with the mashed banana
- Add in baking soda, almond flour, stevia liquid, olive oil, vanilla extract and sea salt.
- Make it a homogenous mass with the aid of a hand blender.
- Open the instant pot and pour in 1 cup of water.
- Carefully place on in the instant pot, the trivet.
- Get the cake pan and pour in the banana mixture and place the pan on the trivet.
- Close the instant pot and set pressure to high. Allow cooking for 60 minutes.
- After the 20 minutes has elapsed, allow pressure to naturally release for 10 minutes and then quick-release. After which, remove from the instant pot.
- Slice to desire and serve.

**Nutrition**: Calories: 54, carbs: 5.5g, Fiber: 0.9g, fat: 3.1g, Protein: 1.9g

# VEGETABLES AND SIDES

# EASY PESTO SPAGHETTI SQUASH

Best paired with perfect Italian meatballs or Simple shredded chicken, this vegetable side can also serve as the main course when topped with a protein dish.

**Serves:** 4

**Time for Preparation:** 3 minutes

**Time for Pressure Cooking:** 7 minutes on High pressure

**Time for Release:** Quick

**Sauté:** 7 minutes

**Total Time:** 27 minutes

**Gluten-free, Vegetarian**

**Ingredients:**

½ cup of pesto

1 diced onion

1 tablespoon of Ghee

1 medium spaghetti squash

2 teaspoons of extra-virgin olive oil

3 sliced Roma tomatoes

Freshly ground black pepper

Sea salt

**Preparation:**

- Cut the spaghetti squash in half then scoop the seeds out with a spoon.
- Get the pressure cooker and pour a cup of water into it, then place the trivet in it. Keep the squash on the trivet, placing the cut-side up.
- Lock the lid and seal it. Adjust pressure to high and time to 7 minutes. Quick release the pressure after cooking. Unlock the lid and remove it.
- Get the squash out of the pot, then use 2 forks to shred it into long strings.
- Get the trivet out and drain the water from the cooker. Choose Browning or Sauté feature then set to medium heat. Include the ghee then add the

onion when it starts to shimmer. Sauté for about 5 minutes till it gets translucent.
- Put in the tomatoes, shredded squash, and pesto then continue to Sauté for 1 or 2 more minutes, till it gets properly heated and mixed. Use pepper and salt to season then drizzle with olive oil.

**Per Serving Contains:** 312 Calories, 9g Total Carbs, 25g Total Fat, 9g Protein, 9g Net Carbs, 3g Sugar, 0g Fiber.

**Macros:** 12% Protein, 76% Fat, and 12% Carbs

## SWEET AND SOUR CABBAGE

**Serves:** 4

**Time for Preparation:** 5 minutes

**Sauté:** 3 minutes

**Time for Pressure Cooking:** 3 minutes on Low pressure

**Time for Release:** Quick

**Total Time:** 23 minutes

**Dairy-free, Nut-free, Gluten-free, and Vegan**

**Ingredients:**

½ minced onion

½ teaspoon of red pepper flakes

¼ cup of coconut oil

¼ cup of full-fat coconut milk

1 tablespoon of onion powder

1 shredded medium head cabbage

1 teaspoon of sea salt, add more as required

3 tablespoons of apple cider vinegar

4 minced garlic cloves

Freshly ground black pepper

6 to 8 drops of liquid stevia or any powdered sugar substitute you prefer which is equal to 1 to 2 tablespoons of sugar (optional)

**Preparation:**

- Choose Sauté or Browning feature on the pressure cooker and set to medium heat. Put the coconut oil in a cooker and heat until it shimmers. Add the garlic and onions then Sauté until the onion gets translucent.
- Add the coconut milk, onion powder, red pepper flakes, cabbage, apple cider vinegar, salt, and stevia (optional) and mix thoroughly.
- Lock the lid securely then set steam to seal. Adjust to low pressure and set time to 3 minutes. Quick release the pressure after cooking. Unlock the lid and remove it then use pepper and salt to season.

**Tip:** If you will like your cabbage soft, naturally release the pressure for about 5 minutes, then quick release the remaining pressure.

**Per Serving Contains:** 122 Calories, 10g Total Carbs, 12g Total Fat, 4g Protein, 4g Net Carbs, 9g Sugar, 3g Fiber.

**Macros:** 10% Protein, 66% Fat, and 24% Carbs

## ASPARAGUS WITH PARMESAN

**Serves:** 4

**Time for Preparation:** 3 minutes

**Time for Pressure Cooking:** 0 minutes on High pressure

**Sauté:** 8 minutes

**Time for Release:** Quick

**Total Time:** 23 minutes

**Gluten-free, Nut-free, Vegetarian**

**Ingredients:**

¼ cup of grated Parmesan cheese

1 teaspoon of dried basil

1 pound of asparagus and trimmed hard ends

2 minced garlic cloves

4 tablespoons of unsalted grass-fed butter

Freshly ground black pepper

Sea salt

**Preparation:**

- Get a pressure cooker and pour 1 cup of water into it then put the steaming rack into it. Place the asparagus on the steaming rack in an even manner.
- Lock the lid and place the steam release knob to sealed position. Set to High pressure and time to 0 minutes. (You can set it to 1 minute if you cannot set to 0 minutes, but be sure to release the pressure when the pot starts counting down.) Quick release the pressure after cooking, then unlock the lid and remove it.
- Remove the steaming rack from the pressure cooker and move the asparagus to a plate. Tent the asparagus with foil to keep it warm them drain the water from the pressure cooker.
- Choose Sauté or Browning feature then set to high heat. Mix the garlic, basil and butter in a pressure cooker. Cook for about 6 to 8 minutes while stirring occasionally. Make sure the butter is browned lightly.
- Place the asparagus on a serving platter. Pour the butter sauce on the asparagus and use Parmesan cheese to sprinkle it. Use pepper and salt to season.

**Per Serving Contains:** 231 Calories, 6g Total Carbs, 19g Total Fat, 12g Protein, 3g Net Carbs, 2g Sugar, 3g Fiber.

**Macros:** 20% Protein, 70% Fat, and 10% Carbs

## COLLARD GREENS

Collard beans are great for a couple of reasons. These antioxidants are rich in vitamins C and K and also contain a lot of fibers. Combined with bacon and garlic, this dish is highly nutritious and tasty.

**Serves:** 5

**Time for Preparation:** 2 minutes

**Sauté:** 8 minutes

**Time for Pressure Cooking:** 20 minutes on High pressure

**Time for Release:** Natural for 5 minutes, then Quick

**Total Time:** 40 minutes

**Dairy-free, Nut-free, and Gluten-free**

**Ingredients:**

½ teaspoon of sea salt

¼ teaspoon of red pepper flakes

1 sliced onion

1 tablespoon of apple cider vinegar

2 cups of chicken broth or bone broth

4 minced garlic cloves

6 cups of chopped collard greens

6 to 9 drops of liquid stevia or 2 tablespoons of any sugar substitute

10 slices of chopped, thick uncured bacon

**Preparation:**

- Choose the Sauté or Browning feature on your pressure cooker then set to medium heat. Put the onion, chopped bacon, and garlic into the pot when it is hot then Sauté for 8 minutes, or until the bacon starts getting crisp.
- Add the apple cider vinegar, bone broth, stevia, collard beans, red pepper flakes, salt to the pot.
- Lock the lid and seal the steam release knob. Adjust pressure to High and time to 20 minutes. Naturally release the pressure for 5 minutes after cooking, then quick release whatever pressure is left. Unlock the lid and remove it.
- Serve hot.

**Per Serving Contains:** 221 Calories, 4g Total Carbs, 15g Total Fat, 15g Protein, 2g Net Carbs, 0g Sugar, 2g Fiber.

**Macros:** 27% Protein, 65% Fat, and 8% Carbs

## PARMESAN ARTICHOKES AND GARLIC AIOLI

Cooking artichokes in a pressure cooker makes them look great and also saves cooking time.

**Serves: 4**

**Time for Preparation: 2 minutes**

**Time for Pressure Cooking: 10 minutes on High**

**Time for Release: Quick**

**Total Time: 22 minutes**

**Gluten-free, Nut-free, Vegetarian**

**Ingredients:**

4 medium artichokes

The juice of 1 divided lemon

¾ cup of grated Parmesan cheese

1 teaspoon of sea salt, add more to taste

1 teaspoon of freshly ground black pepper, add more to taste

¾ cup of avocado oil mayonnaise

2 minced garlic cloves

**Preparation:**

- Cut 1 inch off the top of the artichokes then evenly drizzle ¾ of the lemon juice over them. Spread out the artichoke leaves then inside them sprinkle the Parmesan cheese and 1 teaspoon each of pepper and salt.
- Pour a cup of water into the pressure cooker then put the trivet in it. Neatly place the artichokes on the trivet with their stem-sides down.
- Lock the lid and seal the steam release knob. Adjust pressure to High and time to 10 minutes.

- As the artichokes are cooking, prepare the dipping sauce. Get a small bowl and mix the garlic, mayonnaise, and leftover lemon juice together. Use pepper and salt to season it.
- Pull a leaf of the artichokes from the center and taste to make sure it is soft. If it isn't, lock the lid and cook on high pressure for another 2 to 3 minutes.
- When the artichokes are cooked, quick release the pressure. Unlock the lid and remove it.
- Use tongs to carefully get the artichokes out of the pressure cooker and into plates. Serve along with the dipping sauce.

**Per Serving Contains:** 417 Calories, 7g Total Carbs, 4g Net Carbs, 35g Total Fat, 1g Protein, 3g Sugar, 3g Fiber.

**Macros:** 1% Protein, 81% Fat, and 8% Carbs

## BACON BRUSSELS SPROUTS

Brussels are naturally bitter, but the bacon complements this by adding a very nice sweetness to it. Making this side dish delectable, especially when balsamic vinegar and almonds are added to it.

**Serves:** 6

**Time for Preparation:** 3 minutes

**Time for Pressure Cooking:** 1 minute on High pressure

**Time for Release:** Quick

**Sauté:** 8 minutes

**Total Time:** 25 minutes

**Gluten-free and Dairy-Free**

**Ingredients:**

½ teaspoon of sea salt

¼ cup of sliced almonds

1 teaspoon of onion powder

1 teaspoon of red pepper flakes

2 minced garlic cloves

2 tablespoons of balsamic vinegar

6 thick chopped slices of uncured bacon

16 ounces of trimmed and halved Brussel sprouts

**Preparation:**

- Get your pressure cooker and pour 2 cups of water into it before placing a steamer basket in it. Evenly place the Brussels sprouts in the steamer basket.
- Lock the lid and seal the steam release knob. Adjust pressure to High and time to 1 minute. Quick release the pressure after cooking. Unlock the lid and remove it.
- Get the Brussels sprouts out of the pressure cooker then remove the steamer basket and drain the water from the pressure cooker.
- Choose the Sauté or browning feature on the cooker and set to medium heat. Put in the bacon and cook until it is about to get crisp. Add the Brussels sprouts to the pot, along with the balsamic vinegar, onion powder, garlic, red pepper flakes, almonds, and salt. Stir from time to time while it Sautés for about 6 to 8 minutes. Turn off the pressure cooker when the Brussel sprouts begin to crisp and start getting browned.

**Per Serving Contains:** 181 Calories, 14g Total Carbs, 9g Net Carbs, 11g Total Fat, 8g Protein, 4g Sugar, 5g Fiber.

**Macros:** 21% Protein, 67% Fat, and 12% Carbs

## CAULIFLOWER PUREE

This recipe is a combination of butter, Parmesan cheese, and heavy cream. It is absolutely delicious and easy to prepare.

**Serves: 4**

**Time for Preparation: 3 minutes**

**Time for Pressure Cooking: 3 minutes on High pressure**

**Time for Release: Quick**

**Finishing:** 3 minutes

**Total Time:** 20 minutes

**Gluten-free and Nut-free**

**Ingredients:**

½ teaspoon of freshly ground black pepper

½ teaspoon of sea salt

¼ cup of heavy cream

1 large head cauliflower

1 cup of shredded Parmesan cheese

1 cup of chicken broth or bone broth

4 minced garlic cloves

4 tablespoons of unsalted grass-fed butter, with additional for serving

The green parts of scallions, sliced, for serving

**Preparation:**

- Get the cauliflower's core out, then chop the cauliflower into chunks.
- In the pressure cooker, pour in the bone broth then place the steamer basket inside. Evenly arrange the cauliflower inside the steamer basket.
- Lock the lid and seal the steam release knob. Adjust the pressure level to High and time to 3 minutes. Quick release the pressure after cooking. Unlock the lid and remove it.
- Remove the cauliflower and put it in a food processor. Add the garlic, cream, 4 tablespoons of butter, Parmesan cheese, pepper, and salt to the processor. Process the mixture until it gets very smooth.
- Serve the cauliflower puree alongside some more butter and sliced scallions.

**Tip for Substitution:** If you are avoiding dairy dishes, you can use olive oil instead of butter, and coconut cream instead of heavy cream. Then eliminate the Parmesan cheese.

**Per Serving Contains:** 295 Calories, 10g Total Carbs, 6g Net Carbs, 23g Total Fat, 12g Protein, 4g Sugar, 4g Fiber.

**Macros:** 17% Protein, 70% Fat, and 13% Carbs

## LEMON-GARLIC BROCCOLI

To meet your macro and micronutrient goals, it is better to cook your vegetables in fat and seasonings. The ingredients in this side dish are simple but the results are great for a keto diet.

**Serves:** 5

**Time for Preparation:** 5 minutes

**Time for Pressure Cooking:** 0 minutes on High pressure

**Release:** Quick

**Sauté:** 3 minutes

**Total Time:** 20 minutes

**Gluten-free, Nut-free, and Vegetarian**

**Ingredients:**

Juice of ½ lemon

¼ teaspoon of red pepper flakes

1 teaspoon of sea salt

1 tablespoon of onion powder

3 tablespoons of unsalted grass-fed butter

4 cups of broccoli florets

4 chopped garlic cloves

**Preparation:**

- Pour a cup of water into the pressure cooker then keep the steamer basket in it. Neatly place the broccoli inside the basket.
- Lock the lid properly and seal the steam release knob. Set pressure to High and time to 0 minutes (set on 1 minute if your pressure cooker cannot be set on 0 minutes, but release the pressure when the pot starts counting down). Quick release the pressure after cooking. Unlock the lid and remove it.

- Take the broccoli out of the pressure cooker. Remove the steamer basket and drain the water from the pressure cooker.
- Choose Sauté or Browning on the pressure cooker and set to medium heat. Heat the butter till it foams. Include the garlic and Sauté for about 2 minutes. When it gets lightly browned, include the lemon juice, broccoli, salt, onion powder, and red pepper flakes. Mix properly until the broccoli coats evenly in the seasonings and the butter.
- Move the broccoli to a serving dish then use the butter left in the pressure cooker to drizzle it.

**Per Serving Contains:** 122 Calories, 9g Total Carbs, 6g Net Carbs, 9g Total Fat, 3g Protein, 2g Sugar, 3g Fiber.

**Macros:** 9% Protein, 62% Fat, and 29% Carbs

# SOUPS AND STEWS

# CHUNKY CLAM CHOWDER

**Serves: 8**

**Time for Preparation: 5 minutes**

**Sauté: 10 minutes**

**Time for Pressure Cooking: 5 minutes on High Pressure**

**Time for Release: Quick**

**Total Time: 30 minutes**

**Gluten-free and Nut-free**

**Ingredients:**

½ teaspoon of cayenne pepper (optional)

½ teaspoon of freshly ground black pepper, with extra for seasoning

1 diced onion

1 cup of heavy cream

1 tablespoon of dried thyme

1 (8-ounce) bottle of clam juice

1 teaspoon of sea salt, with extra for seasoning

2 cups of chopped celery

2 cups of bone broth or chicken broth

2 pounds of frozen cauliflower florets

5 (6.5-ounce) cans of chopped and drained clams

6 slices of chopped bacon

6 minced garlic cloves

8 ounces of cream cheese

**Preparation:**

- Choose the Sauté or Browning feature on the pressure cooker then set on medium heat. Put in the bacon then sauté till it gets crisp; this should take

about 6 to 8 minutes. Get the bacon out with the use of a slotted spoon, then put it in a plate lined with paper towel to drain.
- Add the celery, onion and garlic to the fat left of the bacon then sauté for about 3 - 4 minutes.
- Stir in the thyme, clams, broth, cauliflower, clam juice, ½ teaspoon of pepper, 1 teaspoon of salt, and cayenne (if using) until it is properly mixed.
- Lock the lid and seal the steam release knob. Adjust the pressure level to High and time to 5 minutes. Quick release the pressure after cooking, then unlock the lid and remove it.
- Add the cooked bacon, cream cheese, and heavy cream. Keep stirring until the cream cheese melts completely. Season with additional pepper and salt.
- Serve the chowder into different bowls and serve.

**Tip:** After adding the cream, bacon and cream cheese, add 1 or 2 tablespoons of beef gelatin with some tablespoons of cool water or ½ teaspoon of xanthan gum to thicken the soup.

**Per Serving Contains:** 355 Calories, 12g Total Carbs, 8g Net Carbs, 27g Total Fat, 18g Protein, 7g Sugar, 4g Fiber.

**Macros:** 20% Protein, 67% Fat, and 13% Carbs

## THREE-MEAT CHILI

**Serves:** 6

**Time for Preparation:** 5 minutes

**Sauté:** 10 minutes

**Time to Pressure Cook:** 30 minutes on High pressure

**Release:** Quick

**Total Time:** 55 minutes

**Dairy-free, Gluten-free, and Nut-free**

**Ingredients:**

⅓ cup of full-fat coconut cream

¼ cup of chopped fresh cilantro

1 tablespoon of chili powder

1 diced green bell pepper

1 pound of uncured, chopped bacon

1 pound of hot Italian sausage

1 tablespoon of ground cumin

1 (8-ounce) can of tomato paste

1 cup of bone broth or beef broth

1 tablespoon of smoked paprika

1 pound of grass-fed ground beef

1 avocado, halved, pitted, peeled, and sliced

2 yellow diced onions

2 (14.5-ounce) cans of diced tomatoes with their juices

5 minced garlic cloves

**Preparation:**

- Choose the Sauté or Browning feature on the pressure cooker then set to medium heat. Place the bacon inside and cook until it becomes crisp, while stirring frequently. Remove the bacon with a slotted spoon, but leave the fat in the pot.
- Add the green pepper, onions, and garlic to the fat in the cooker and Sauté for 3 to 5 minutes. Put in the diced tomatoes with their juices, sausage, beef, bone broth, tomato paste, smoked paprika, chili powder, and cumin. Cook for 3 to 5 minutes while stirring occasionally.
- Put the bacon back into the pressure cooker. Lock the lid and seal the steam release knob. Adjust the pressure level to High and time to 30 minutes. Quick release the pressure after cooking, then unlock the lid and remove it.
- Spoon the chili into bowls and garnish with the chopped coconut cream, cilantro, avocado slices. Serve.

**Per Serving Contains:** 612 Calories, 16g Total Carbs, 12g Net Carbs, 45g Total Fat, 33g Protein, 6g Sugar, 3g Fiber.

**Macros:** 22% Protein, 68% Fat, and 10% Carbs

# ROASTED TOMATO SOUP

**Serves:** 5

**Time for Preparation:** 5 minutes

**Sauté:** 12 minutes

**Time for Pressure Cooking:** 3 minutes on High pressure

**Time for Release:** 10 minutes for Natural, then Quick

**Total Time:** 45 minutes

**Gluten-free and Nut-free**

**Ingredients:**

3 pounds of Roma tomatoes, to be cut lengthwise

2 tablespoons of avocado oil

Sea salt

Freshly ground black pepper

3 tablespoons of unsalted grass-fed butter

1 head of garlic, the cloves should be separated and peeled

1 yellow minced onion

1 medium shredded carrot

2 cups of bone broth or chicken broth

2 tablespoons of coconut aminos

¼ cup of oil-packed tomatoes, sun-dried, drained, and chopped

1 cup of chopped fresh basil

1 teaspoon of dried thyme

½ cup of heavy cream

½ cup of cream cheese

**Preparation:**

- Get the oven preheated to broil.
- Place the tomatoes with their cut-side up on a baking sheet. Use avocado oil to drizzle then season with pepper and salt. Place the tomatoes very close to the broiler element to cook for about 3 to 5 minutes. Stop cooking and remove from the oven when you see blackened spots. Allow to cool a bit.
- Choose Sauté or Browning feature on the pressure cooker, then set heat to medium and place your butter in it to melt until it begins to foam. Add the cloves of garlic and cook for 4 to 5 minutes. When they begin to turn a golden brown, add the carrot and onion and Sauté for 3 to 4 minutes.
- Add the sun-dried tomatoes, thyme, broth, basil, roasted tomatoes, and coconut aminos.
- Lock the lid and adjust the pressure level to High and time to 3 minutes. Naturally release the pressure for 10 minutes after cooking. Quick release any pressure left.
- Blend the soup in an immersion blender until it becomes very smooth. You can also put the soup in a blender in small batches and blend until smooth before returning the soup to the cooker.
- Add the cream cheese and heavy cream and stir properly till the cream cheese melts completely. Use pepper and salt to season. Scoop into bowls and serve.

**Cooking Tip:** You can use 1 to 2 tablespoons of powdered sugar in place of tomatoes, or 6 – 8 drop of liquid stevia so that the acidity level can be balanced.

**Per Serving Contains:** 317 Calories, 13g Total Carbs, 8g Net Carbs, 24g Total Fat, 7g Protein, 5g Sugar, 5g Fiber.

**Macros:** 10% Protein, 73% Fat, and 17% Carbs

# BEEF STEW

**Serves: 6**

**Time for Preparation: 10 minutes**

**Sauté: 5 minutes**

**Time for Pressure Cooking: 35 minutes on High Pressure**

**Time for Release:** Quick

**Total Time:** 1 hour

**Dairy-free, Gluten-free, and Nut-free**

**Ingredients:**

½ cup of bone broth or beef broth

¾ cup of red wine

¼ cup of chopped fresh parsley

1 teaspoon of dried thyme

1 pound of quartered mushrooms

1 teaspoon of dried oregano

1 teaspoon of freshly ground black pepper, add more for seasoning

2 bay leaves

2 sliced onions

2 tablespoons of tomato paste

2 teaspoons of coarse sea salt, divided

2 pounds of grass-fed chuck roast or beef brisket, to be cut into 2-inch chunks

3 tablespoons of avocado oil

6 garlic cloves, sliced

**Preparation:**

- Get a large bowl and toss in the beef along with a teaspoon of pepper and 1 ½ teaspoons of coarse sea salt. Set aside.
- Choose the Sauté or Browning feature on the pressure cooker and set the heat to medium. Place the avocado oil in the cooker to heat until it shimmers then add mushrooms, garlic, and onions. Cook for about 5 minutes, stirring from time to time until the onions turn translucent. Add the red wine, tomato paste, oregano, broth, beef, bay leaves, and thyme and mix properly.

- Lock the lid securely and seal the steam release knob. Set to High pressure and adjust time to 35 minutes. Quick release the pressure after cooking. Unlock the lid and remove it.
- Remove the bay leaves and use the remaining ½ teaspoon of salt and additional pepper to season the stew. Scoop into bowls, garnish with the chopped parsley, then serve.

**Per Serving Contains:** 509 Calories, 8g Total Carbs, 5g Net Carbs, 33g Total Fat, 32g Protein, 2g Sugar, 3g Fiber.

**Macros:** 28% Protein, 65% Fat, and 7% Carbs

## TOM KHA GAI

**Serves:** 5

**Time for Preparation:** 5 minutes

**Time for Pressure Cooking:** 10 minutes on High pressure

**Time of Release:** 10 minutes of natural, then Quick

**Total Time:** 35 minutes

**Dairy-free, Gluten-free, and Nut-free**

**Ingredients:**

¼ cup of chopped fresh cilantro

¼ cup of freshly squeezed lime juice

1 tablespoon of red chili paste

1 tablespoon of sweet dried basil

1 tablespoon of finely grated lime zest

1½ pounds of boneless, skinless chicken breasts

2 bay leaves

2 tablespoons of fish sauce

2 cups of Bone Broth or chicken broth

2 scallions, green parts only, sliced

2 (13.5-ounce) cans of full-fat coconut milk

2 tablespoons of peeled minced fresh ginger

2 stalks of lemongrass, tough outer layers removed, chopped into 4-inch pieces

4 cups of sliced mushrooms

Freshly ground black pepper

Sea salt

Lime wedges, for serving

**Preparation:**

- Put the chicken, coconut milk, broth, lemongrass, lime juice, lime zest, ginger, bay leaves, fish sauce, basil, mushrooms, scallions, and chili paste together in the pressure cooker and stir properly.
- Lock the lid properly and seal the steam release knob. Set pressure to High and time to 10 minutes. Naturally release the pressure for 10 minutes after cooking, then quick release whatever pressure is left. Unlock the lid and remove it.
- Use a slotted spoon to get the lemongrass and bay leaves out of the pot, then get rid of them. Make use of same slotted spoon to move the chicken to a plate before cutting it into bite-size pieces. Put the chicken back into the soup and add the chopped cilantro to the pot. Stir to properly mix, then use pepper and salt to season.
- Serve with lime wedges inside soup bowls.

**Preparation Tip:** Get rid of the loose outer layers of the lemongrass stalks while preparing them. Cut the lower white parts of the lemongrass into 4-inch sections. Smash the lemongrass with a knife to release its flavor before you add them to the soup.

**Per Serving Contains:** 417 Calories, 10g Total Carbs, 9g Net Carbs, 29g Total Fat, 32g Protein, 4g Sugar, 1g Fiber.

**Macros:** 30% Protein, 61% Fat, and 9% Carbs

# ROASTED GARLIC CAULIFLOWER SOUP

**Serves:** 4

**Time for Preparation:** 5 minutes

**Sauté:** 15 minutes

**Time for Pressure Cooking:** 8 minutes on High pressure

**Release:** Quick

**Total Time:** 30 minutes

**Gluten-free and Nut-free**

**Ingredients:**

½ cup of full-fat coconut cream

¼ teaspoon of freshly ground black pepper

1 diced carrot

1 diced onion

1 teaspoon of sea salt

1 teaspoon of ground cumin

1 teaspoon of ground turmeric

1 teaspoon of dried oregano

1 teaspoon of peeled minced fresh ginger

1 head of garlic, with their cloves separated and peeled

2 tablespoons of avocado oil

3 tablespoons of Ghee

3 tablespoons of chopped fresh parsley

4 cups of bone broth or chicken broth

6 cups of cauliflower florets

**Preparation:**

- Choose Sauté or Browning on the pressure cooker and set on low heat. Put the avocado oil and ghee into the cooker and heat until the ghee melts.
- Add the garlic then cook for about 10 minutes, while seldom stirring, until the cloves turn a golden brown. Include the carrot and onion and Sauté for 5 minutes. Afterward, add the ginger, oregano, cauliflower, turmeric, broth, cumin, pepper, and salt to the pot.
- Lock the lid and seal the steam release knob. Set on High pressure and adjust time to 10 minutes. Quick release the pressure after cooking then unlock the lid and remove it.
- Blend the soup in an immersion blender until it is generally smooth (you can use a general blender, but make sure you blend in batches). Pour the soup back into the pressure cooker after blending.
- Spoon the soup into 4 bowls. Stir the coconut cream and use parsley to garnish it. For increased protein content, top with some simple shredded chicken. Serve.

**Per Serving Contains:** 370 Calories, 15g Total Carbs, 10g Net Carbs, 28g Total Fat, 18g Protein, 10g Sugar, 5g Fiber.

**Macros:** 12% Protein, 71% Fat, and 17% Carbs

## WHITE CHICKEN CHILI

Dairy lovers will love this soup. It comprises heavy cream, sour cream, cream cheese, and a topping of shredded cheese. The meal is absolutely delicious.

**Serves:** 6

**Time for Preparation:** 5 minutes

**Sauté:** 8 minutes

**Time for Pressure Cooking:** 10 minutes on High pressure

**Time for Release:** 10 minutes on Natural, then Quick

**Total Time:** 42 minutes

**Gluten-free and Nut-free**

**Ingredients:**

½ cup of heavy cream

½ cup of sour cream

½ cup of cream cheese

½ cup of shredded Cheddar cheese

¼ cup of chopped fresh cilantro

1 diced onion

1 lime, cut into wedges

1 teaspoon of ground cumin

1 teaspoon of chili powder

1 (4-ounce) can of green chiles

1 teaspoon of dried oregano

1 teaspoon of freshly ground black pepper

1½ pounds of boneless, skinless chicken thighs

2 teaspoons of sea salt

2 tablespoons of unsalted grass-fed butter

2 avocados, halved, pitted, peeled, and diced

3 cups of bone broth or chicken broth

4 minced garlic cloves

**Preparation:**
- Choose Sauté or Browning on the pressure cooker and set heat to medium. Put the butter in the cooker and let it melt till it foams. Add the garlic and onion and let it Sauté for about 4 minutes, pending when the onion gets translucent.
- Put in the chicken and brown all sides for 2 to 3 minutes. Include the oregano, chiles, cumin, chili powder, broth, pepper, and salt.
- Lock the lid properly and seal the steam release knob. Set to High pressure and set time to 10 minutes. Naturally release the pressure for 10 minutes after cooking, then quick release whatever pressure is left. Unlock the lid and remove it. Use a slotted spoon to take out the chicken thighs and place them

on a plate. Shred the meat with two forks before placing them back into the pressure cooker.
- Add the cream cheese, sour cream, and heavy cream to the pot and mix until the cream cheese melts.
- Spoon the chili in bowls and top with the shredded cheese, diced avocado, lime wedges, and chopped cilantro.

**Per Serving Contains:** 509 Calories, 11g Total Carbs, 7g Net Carbs, 37g Total Fat, 30g Protein, 4g Sugar, 4g Fiber.

**Macros:** 25% Protein, 67% Fat, and 8% Carbs

## HUNGARIAN MUSHROOM SOUP

**Serves:** 4

**Time for Preparation:** 5 minutes

**Sauté:** 10 minutes

**Time for Pressure Cooking:** 20 minutes on High pressure

**Release:** Quick

**Total Time:** 55 minutes

**Gluten-free and Nut-free**

**Ingredients:**

½ cup of sour cream

½ cup of heavy cream

½ cup of dry white wine

¼ cup of chopped fresh parsley

1 teaspoon of sea salt

1 tablespoon of paprika

1 pound of sliced mushrooms

1 tablespoon of coconut aminos

2 cups of sliced onions

2 teaspoons of dried dill weed

2 cups of bone broth or chicken broth

2 teaspoons of freshly squeezed lemon juice

3 minced garlic cloves

3 tablespoons of unsalted grass-fed butter

Freshly ground black pepper

**Preparation:**

- Choose Sauté or Browning on your pressure cooker and set to medium heat. Melt the butter inside the pot until it foams then add the garlic and onions to Sauté for another 3 to 5 minutes. When the onions are translucent, add the mushrooms as well as salt and Sauté for additional 5 minutes. Take out ½ cup of mushrooms and set it aside.
- Add the coconut aminos, broth, dill, wine, and paprika to the cooker and combine properly.
- Lock the lid securely and seal the steam release knob. Set pressure to High and time to 20 minutes. Quick release all the pressure after cooking then unlock the lid and remove it.
- Blend in an immersion blender or regular blender (in batches) until it is smooth. Include the heavy cream and blend until it mixes properly. Return the soup to the pressure cooker if a regular blender was used.
- Add the sour cream parsley, lemon juice, and ½ cup of mushrooms reserved earlier. Mix properly and use pepper to season the soup.
- Ladle the soup into bowls and serve.

**Substitution of Ingredient:** If you are going dairy-free, you could use dairy-free sour cream instead of sour cream, and coconut cream instead of heavy cream.

**Per Serving Contains:** 331 Calories, 15g Total Carbs, 12g Net Carbs, 18.5g Total Fat, 8g Protein, 7g Sugar, 3g Fiber.

**Macros:** 10% Protein, 72% Fat, and 18% Carbs

# PUMPKIN-COCONUT SOUP

Pumpkin is high in carbs so be careful with the size while serving this recipe.

**Serves:** 5

**Time for Preparation:** 3 minutes

**Sauté:** 5 minutes

**Time for Pressure Cooking:** 10 minutes on High pressure

**Release:** 10 minutes for Natural, then Quick

**Total Time:** 38 minutes

**Dairy-free, Gluten-free, and nut-free**

**Ingredients:**

¼ cup of chopped fresh cilantro

¼ cup of toasted pumpkin seeds

½ teaspoon of ground cloves

½ teaspoon of freshly ground black pepper, with additional for seasoning

1 diced onion

1 teaspoon of curry powder

1 teaspoon of ground nutmeg

1 tablespoon of freshly squeezed lime juice

1 (13.5-ounce) can of full-fat coconut cream

1 tablespoon of peeled minced fresh ginger

2 cups of pumpkin purée

2 tablespoons of coconut oil

2 teaspoons of ground cinnamon

2 cups of bone broth or chicken broth

2 teaspoons of sea salt, plus more for seasoning

4 minced garlic cloves

4 to 6 drops of liquid stevia or use powdered sugar substitute equivalent to 1 to 2 teaspoons sugar (optional)

**Preparation:**

- Choose Sauté or Browning on the pressure cooker then set heat to Medium. Heat the coconut oil inside until it shimmers. Include the onion and cook for about 5 minutes till it gets tender. Include the ginger and garlic then cook for about a minute while stirring constantly until it gets fragrant.
- Stir the cinnamon, cloves, curry powder, nutmeg, ½ teaspoon of pepper, as well as 2 teaspoons of salt in the pot. Include the broth and pumpkin puree and whisk properly until it is perfectly mixed.
- Lock the lid securely and seal the steam release knob. Set pressure to High and time to 10 minutes. Naturally release the pressure for 10 minutes after cooking, then quick release whatever pressure is left. Unlock the lid and remove it.
- Blend in an immersion blender until it becomes smooth. If using a regular blender, blend until it is smooth then return the soup to the pressure cooker.
- Return the pressure cooker to Sauté or Browning setting then include the lime juice, coconut cream, and stevia (optional). Stir well until it is properly mixed and heated. Add more pepper and salt to season.
- Ladle into bowls and garnish with cilantro and toasted pumpkin seeds. Serve.

**Per Serving Contains:** 215 Calories, 13g Total Carbs, 2g Net Carbs, 16g Total Fat, 5g Protein, 6g Sugar, 11g Fiber.

**Macros:** 8% Protein, 67% Fat, and 25% Carbs

## KALE AND SAUSAGE SOUP

This combination of kale and Italian sausage is both delightful and comforting. If you are on a dairy-free diet, replace the heavy cream with coconut milk and so not use the Parmesan cheese.

**Serves:** 5

**Time for Preparation:** 5 minutes

**Sauté:** 5 minutes

**Time for Pressure Cooking: 5 minutes on High pressure**

**Time for Release: 10 minutes for Natural, then Quick**

**Total Time: 35 minutes**

**Gluten-free and Nut-free**

**Ingredients:**

½ cup of grated Parmesan cheese

¼ teaspoon of freshly ground black pepper, add more for seasoning

1 cup of diced tomatoes

1 minced medium onion

1 pound of Italian sausage

1 teaspoon of dried oregano

1 cup of heavy cream or full-fat coconut milk

1 teaspoon of sea salt, add more for seasoning

4 cups of bone broth or chicken broth

6 minced garlic cloves

6 cups of chopped kale

**Preparation:**

- Choose Sauté or Browning and set heat to medium. Place the sausage inside the pot and crumble it with a wooden spoon. ¼ teaspoon of pepper, broth, garlic, onion, 1 teaspoon of salt, tomatoes, and oregano. Cook them for about 5 minutes and make sure the sausage is browned and the onions are translucent.
- Lock the lid securely then seal the steam release knob. Set the pressure to High and the time to 5 minutes. Naturally release the pressure for 10 minutes, then quick release whatever pressure is left. Unlock the lid and remove it.
- Stir the Cream, Parmesan cheese, and kale into the pot and keep stirring until the kale gets soft. Use additional pepper and salt to season. Scoop into bowls and serve.

**Per Serving Contains:** 523 Calories, 15g Total Carbs, 10g Net Carbs, 37g Total Fat, 27g Protein, 6g Sugar, 5g Fiber.

**Macros:** 21% Protein, 67% Fat, and 12% Carbs

## NO-NOODLE CHICKEN SOUP

**Serves:** 4

**Time for Preparation:** 3 minutes

**Sauté:** 5 minutes

**Time for Pressure Cook:** 10 minutes on High, with additional 2 minutes on High

**Release:** Quick

**Total Time:** 30 minutes

**Gluten-free and Nut-free**

**Ingredients:**

1 chopped onion

1 teaspoon of dried oregano

1 teaspoon of freshly ground black pepper, with additional for seasoning

1 to 2 tablespoons of beef gelatin or ¼ to ½ teaspoon of xanthan gum

1½ pounds of boneless, skinless chicken thighs

2 teaspoons of dried thyme

2 cups of chopped cabbage

2 teaspoons of freshly squeezed lemon juice

3 sliced carrots

3 tablespoons of Ghee

3 teaspoons of sea salt, with additional for seasoning

4 minced garlic cloves

4 chopped celery stalks

6 cups of bone broth or chicken broth

**Preparation:**

- Choose Sauté or Browning and set to medium heat. Put the ghee inside and heat until it shimmers. Include the onion and garlic then Sauté for about 5 minutes, till the onion gets translucent.
- Put in the broth, chicken, 1 teaspoon of pepper, and 3 teaspoons of salt. Lock the lid securely and seal the steam release knob. Quick release the pressure after cooking then unlock the lid and remove it.
- Use a slotted spoon to get the chicken out of the pot and place it on a plate. Use two forks to shred the meat. Place the chicken in the pressure cooker.
- Gr Put the carrots, thyme, oregano, celery, and cabbage in the pot. Lock the lid securely and seal the steam release knob. Adjust the pressure to High and set time to 2 minutes. Quick release the pressure after cooking. Unlock the lid before removing it.
- To make the soup thicker, mix a tablespoon of gelatin with some tablespoons of cool water till they dissolve, then allow to sit for 1 minute. Slowly add the soup until it is as thick as you want it (although it will thicken while it cools). You can add more gelatin mixed with water as desired. If you are using zanthan gum, stir in ¼ teaspoon until it gets to a consistency you want.
- Add the lemon juice and use pepper and salt to season the soup. Serve in four bowls.

**Per Serving Contains:** 482 Calories, 12g Total Carbs, 3g Net Carbs, 29g Total Fat, 48g Protein, 5g Sugar, 9g Fiber.

**Macros:** 39% Protein, 52% Fat, and 9% Carbs

# POULTRY, FISH, AND SHELLFISH

## LOBSTER TAIL SALAD

In this recipe, lobster meat pairs beautifully with shallots, avocado and lemon. The delicate and sweetened flavor of the lobster goes well with the fresh beans and drizzle of olive oil. This meal is rich in flavor and contains a lot of fats.

**Serves:** 4

**Time for Preparation:** 5 minutes

**Time for Pressure Cooking:** 4 minutes on high pressure

**Release:** Quick

**Total Time:** 20 minutes, with 30 minutes for chilling

**Gluten-free, Dairy-free, and Nut-free**

**Ingredients:**

½ cup of Avocado Oil Mayonnaise, avocado oil bought from a store, or olive oil mayonnaise

¼ teaspoon of celery salt

¼ cup of chopped shallots

¼ teaspoon of freshly ground black pepper, with extra for seasoning

1½ cups of chicken stock

2 pounds of lobster tails

2 cups of mixed greens or lettuce leaves

2 avocados, halved, pitted, peeled, and sliced

2 tablespoons of finely chopped fresh tarragon

4 tablespoons of extra-virgin olive oil

Sea salt

Juice from 1½ lemons, divided

**Preparation:**

- Use a chef's knife to cut the lobster tails lengthwise in half. Pour the chicken stock into the cooker then keep the trivet inside it. Place the lobster tails, with

- their shell-side down, on the trivet. Squeeze about 1/3 of the lemon juice on the lobster.
- Secure the lid and sea the steam release knob. Adjust the pressure to High and time to 4 minutes.
- As the lobster is cooking, mix the tarragon, mayonnaise, ¼ teaspoon of pepper, shallots, and celery salt together in a medium bowl. Get a larger bowl and fill it with cold water.
- When the lobster is cooked, quick release the pressure. Unlock the lid and remove it. Use tongs to carefully move the lobster tails from the pot to a bowl of cold water so that it will stop cooking.
- Take out the meat from the lobster shells and chop them into small chunks as soon as the lobster is cool enough to handle. Put these meat chunks into the mayonnaise mixture and mix. Place in a refrigerator to chill for 30 minutes.
- When it is cool, prepare a bed of mixed greens and place the lobster salad on top. Top this up with slices of avocado and drizzle with olive oil. Use pepper and salt to season it to taste.

**Per Serving Contains:** 583 Calories, 10g Total Carbs, 4g Net Carbs, 38g Total Fat, 46g Protein, 1g Sugar, 6g Fiber.

**Macros:** 32% Protein, 61% Fat, and 7% Carbs

## MUSSELS WITH GARLIC AND WINE

The combination of butter, garlic, and wine with mussels will boost the shellfish flavor instead of overpowering it. This meal has an amazing taste and is highly nutritious.

**Serves:** 4

**Time for Preparation:** 3 minutes

**Sauté:** 9 minutes

**Time for Pressure Cooking:** 3 minutes on High pressure

**Release:** Quick

**Total Time:** 25 minutes

**Gluten-free and Nut-free**

**Ingredients:**

Sea salt

¼ cup of chopped fresh parsley

1 sliced shallot

1 cup of dry white wine

1 tablespoon of dried thyme

1 tablespoon of avocado oil

1 tablespoon of dried oregano

2 pounds of mussels in shells, rinsed and debearded

3 tablespoons of unsalted grass-fed butter, divided

6 minced garlic cloves

Freshly ground black pepper

**Preparation:**

- Choose the Sauté or Browning feature on the pressure cooker then set heat to high. Pour the avocado oil into the cooker and heat until it shimmers before adding the shallot and seasoning with pepper and salt. Sauté until the shallot starts turning brown, this should take about 5 minutes. Add 1 tablespoon of butter and garlic then Sauté for a minute or 2. Thereafter, add the wine, oregano, and thyme then allow to simmer for 2 minutes.
- Put in the mussels. Close the lid, lock it, then seal the steam release knob. Set pressure to High and time to 3 minutes. Quick release the pressure after cooking. Unlock the lid and remove it. Then use a slotted spoon to remove the mussels from the pot and into serving bowls. Get rid of any mussel that is not opened.
- Mix the parsley with the leftover 2 tablespoons of butter in the pressure pot. Stir properly until the butter melts. Pour this sauce on the mussels, season with pepper and salt, then serve.

**Ingredients:** Scrub the mussels very well and soak them before cooking if you had to harvest them yourself or purchased wild ones.

**Per Serving Contains:** 261 Calories, 8g Total Carbs, 7g Net Carbs, 15g Total Fat, 14g Protein, 1g Sugar, 1g Fiber.

**Macros:** 26% Protein, 60% Fat, and 14% Carbs

## HERB AND LEMON SALMON

This salmon, well loaded with lemon, herbs, and garlic, is nutrient-rich and has a texture that will melt in your mouth in an amazing manner.

**Serves:** 4

**Time for Preparation:** 7 minutes

**Time for Pressure Cooking:** 3 minutes on High pressure

**Release:** Quick

**Total Time:** 20 minutes

**Dairy-free, Nut-free, and Gluten-free**

**Ingredients:**

¾ cup of Avocado Oil Mayonnaise or store-bought olive oil or avocado oil mayonnaise

1 tablespoon of minced garlic

1 tablespoon of finely grated lemon zest

1 tablespoon of freshly squeezed lemon juice

1 pound of wild-caught Alaskan salmon fillet, cut into four pieces

2 teaspoons of sea salt

3 tablespoons of chopped fresh parsley, divided

**Preparation:**

- Mix the 2 tablespoons of parsley, mayonnaise, lemon zest, lemon juice, garlic, and salt in a small bowl. Keep each salmon piece on an aluminum foil piece, with the skin side down. Spread the mixture of mayonnaise on the salmon in an even manner then wrap to seal each.
- Pour a cup of water into the pressure cooker and put the trivet in it. Arrange each of the wrapped foils on the trivet.

- Lock the lid and seal the steam release knob. Set pressure to High and time to 3 minutes. Then quick release the pressure after cooking.
- Unlock the lid and remove it. Take out the salmon packets from the cooker.
- Unwrap the salmon and use a tablespoon of parsley to sprinkle it evenly. Serve instantly.

**Cooking Tip:** The time taken to cook the salmon fillets will depend on how thick and big the fillets are. Fillets of about 1-inch thickness will require about 3 minutes to cook.

**Per Serving Contains:** 302 Calories, 7g Total Carbs, 4g Net Carbs, 19g Total Fat, 23g Protein, 0g Sugar, 3g Fiber.

**Macros:** 31% Protein, 60% Fat, and 9% Carbs

## SNAPPER VERACRUZ

This traditional Mexico dish is spicy and flavor-rich. It is combined with tomatoes, jalapenos, savory herbs, and onions to make the perfect entrée for your quick dinner.

**Serves:** 4

**Time for Preparation:** 10 minutes

**Time for Pressure Cook:** 5 minutes on high pressure, with 1 minute on High pressure

**Release:** Quick, 2 minutes Natural, and Quick

**Total Time:** 30 minutes

**Dairy-free, Gluten-free, and Nut-free**

**Ingredients:**

½ teaspoon dried oregano

½ small onion, sliced (about ½ cup)

¼ cup sliced green olives

1 bay leaf

1 (14.5-ounce) can diced tomatoes, drained

1 small jalapeño pepper, seeded and minced (about 1 tablespoon)

2 large garlic cloves, minced

2 tablespoons chopped fresh parsley, divided

3 tablespoons capers, divided

4 snapper fillets, about 5 ounces each

5 tablespoons extra-virgin olive oil, divided

Kosher salt

Freshly ground black pepper

**Preparation:**

- Place the snapper fillets on a plate and season with pepper and salt. Place them in the refrigerator as you prepare the sauce.
- Select Sauté or Brown on the pressure cooker then set on high heat. Place 4 tablespoons of olive oil in the cooker and heat until it shimmers. Include the onion then sprinkle with 1 or 2 pinches of salt. Cook for about 5 minutes, while stirring until the onion gets brown. Add jalapeno and garlic for a minute or 2, until the garlic gets fragrant and most of the onion is browned.
- Add the oregano, tomatoes, 1½ tablespoons of capers, bay leaf, 1 tablespoon of parsley, and olives and mix properly.
- Lock the lid securely and seal the steam release knob. Set on high pressure and adjust time to 5 minutes. Quick release the pressure after cooking. Unlock the lid and remove it.
- Take the snapper out of the refrigerator and put the fillets on the sauce. Lock the lid securely and seal the steam release knob. Set on high pressure and adjust time to 1 minute. Naturally release the pressure for 2 minutes after cooking, then quick release whatever pressure is left. Unlock the lid and remove it.
- Use a fork to check the fish and ensure that the center is cooked. If it is not cooked, place the lid back on the cooker without locking it, then allow the fish to cook for additional 1 to 2 minutes. (The steam and residual heat will finish cooking the fish.)
- Keep the snapper fillets on a serving platter and put the sauce on it. Sprinkle the top with a tablespoon of olive oil, 1½ tablespoons of capers, and the 1 tablespoon of parsley left.

**Per Serving Contains:** 343 Calories, 7g Total Carbs, 2g Net Carbs, 20g Total Fat, 30g Protein, 3g Sugar, 5g Fiber.

**Macros:** 36% Protein, 55% Fat, and 9% Carbs

## JAMBALAYA

This keto dish is a delightful combination of spicy sausage, Cajun spices, and seafood. To keep the carb content low, cauliflower was used in place of traditional rice.

**Serves:** 8

**Time for Preparation:** 5 minutes

**Sauté:** 8 minutes

**Time for Pressure Cooking:** 2 minutes on High pressure

**Release:** Quick

**Total Time:** 25 minutes

**Gluten-free and Nut-free**

**Ingredients:**

½ teaspoon of cayenne pepper

1 sliced zucchini

1 cup of dry white wine

1 cup of chopped onion

1 cup of chopped celery

1 tablespoon of dried thyme

1 large head of cauliflower, separated into florets

1 tablespoon of ground cumin

1 tablespoon of minced garlic

1 tablespoon of onion powder

1 tablespoon of smoked paprika

1 cup of chopped green bell pepper

1 teaspoon of Worcestershire sauce

1 pound of sliced andouille sausage

1 pound of peeled and deveined shrimp

1 (14.5-ounce) can of diced tomatoes with their juices

1 pound of boneless, skinless chicken thighs, chopped

1½ teaspoons of sea salt

2 tablespoons of chopped fresh parsley

3 sliced scallions, green parts only

4 tablespoons of Ghee, divided

**Preparation:**

- Pulse the cauliflower in a food processor until it breaks down into pieces that are rice-sized. Take out the cauliflower and put it aside.
- Choose the Sauté or Browning feature on the pressure cooker then set heat on high. Put a tablespoon of ghee inside the cooker to melt. Put in the shrimp and Sauté each side for few minutes, till the shrimp become opaque. Thereafter, use a slotted spoon to move the shrimp to a plate before setting it aside.
- Melt the 3 tablespoons of ghee left in the pressure cooker. Include onion, celery, chicken, zucchini, garlic, sausage, and bell pepper then Sauté for about 4 minutes. Add the smoked paprika, cayenne, thyme, salt, cumin, Worcestershire sauce, white wine, and onion powder then allow to simmer for a minute or 2.
- Add the tomatoes along with their juices then stir until it is mixed.
- Lock the lid then seal the steam release knob. Adjust the pressure to High and the time to 2 minutes. Quick release the pressure after cooking. Unlock the lid and remove it.
- Choose Sauté or Browning on the pressure cooker again then set heat on high. Gently stir in the riced cauliflower, continue stirring while it cooks for about 5 to 6 minutes. When the cauliflower reaches the consistency you prefer, add the shrimp and mix well.

- Scoop into bowls then use the sliced scallion greens and chopped parsley to garnish. Serve.

**Ingredient Tip:** Use andouille sausage and fresh shrimp to get great flavor. You can also use frozen shrimp that is cooked on high pressure for 1 minute. Either kielbasa or chorizo can also be used in place of andouille sausage.

**Per Serving Contains:** 406 Calories, 15g Total Carbs, 11g Net Carbs, 25g Total Fat, 27g Protein, 8g Sugar, 4g Fiber.

**Macros:** 28% Protein, 57% Fat, and 15% Carbs

# SHRIMP SCAMPI

**Serves:** 4

**Time for Preparation:** 5 minutes

**Sauté:** 4 minutes

**Time for Pressure Cooking:** 1 minute on High pressure

**Release:** Quick

**Total Time:** 20 minutes

**Gluten-free and Nut-free**

**Ingredients:**

½ cup of dry white wine

½ cup of grated Parmesan cheese

1 teaspoon of sea salt

1 teaspoon of finely grated lemon zest

1 teaspoon of freshly ground black pepper

1 pound of frozen shrimp, peeled and deveined

2 tablespoons of chopped fresh parsley

3 minced shallots

3 cups of Zucchini Noodles

4 tablespoons of unsalted grass-fed butter

4 tablespoons of minced garlic

Juice of 1 lemon

**Preparation:**

- Choose Sauté or Browning on the pressure cooker. Set on high heat and melt the butter until it foams. Include the shallots and garlic to the pot then Sauté for about 2 minutes. Once it gets browned, add the white wine then cook for a minute a 2, till the alcohol burns off.
- Add the pepper, frozen shrimp, lemon juice, and salt to the pot then stir to mix. Lock the lid and seal the steam release knob. Set to High pressure and time to 1 minute. Quick release the pressure after cooking, then unlock the lid and remove it.
- Choose Sauté or Browning on the pressure cooker again then set to high heat. Add the Parmesan cheese and lemon zest to the shrimp and mix thoroughly. Place on the zucchini noodles and use the chopped parsley to garnish. Serve immediately.

**Cooking Tip:** Due to the fact that shrimp cooks pretty fast in a pressure cooker, it is important to set the timer to 0 so you will not overcook them.

**Per Serving Contains:** 417 Calories, 10g Total Carbs, 9g Net Carbs, 26g Total Fat, 35g Protein, 2g Sugar, 1g Fiber.

**Macros:** 34% Protein, 56% Fat, and 10% Carbs

## SIMPLE SALMON AND BROCCOLINI

This dish, made with simple ingredients, is nutrient-rich and will be ready in less than 30 minutes.

**Serves:** 4

**Time for Preparation:** 2 minutes

**Time for Pressure Cooking:** 3 minutes on High, additional 0 minutes on Low

**Release:** Quick

**Total Time:** 15 minutes

**Gluten-free and Nut-free**

**Ingredients:**

Sea salt

¼ cup of unsalted grass-fed butter, add 2 tablespoons melted

1 tablespoon of onion powder

2 teaspoons of chopped fresh dill

4 minced garlic cloves

4 (4- to 6-ounce) fillets of frozen wild-caught Alaskan salmon

8 ounces of broccolini

Freshly ground black pepper

**Preparation:**

- Evenly apply the dill and garlic on the salmon then season with pepper and salt. Get the pressure cooker and pour a cup of water into it before placing the trivet inside. Assemble the salmon on the trivet. Each of the salmon fillets should have a tablespoon of butter placed on top.
- Shut the lid, lock it properly, then seal the steam release knob. Set on High pressure and adjust time to 3 minutes. Quick release the pressure after cooking. Unlock the lid and remove it.
- Evenly arrange the broccolini on the salmon. Season with salt, pepper, and onion powder. Lock the lid and seal the steam release knob. Set on Low pressure and adjust time to 0 minutes.
- Quick release the pressure after cooking then take out the broccolini and salmon. Serve this dish with the 2 tablespoons of melted butter left.

**Ingredient Tip:** Regular broccoli can be used in place of broccolini. If fresh salmon is being used, cut the cook time down to 1 or 2 minutes on High.

**Per Serving (1 Fillet) Contains:** 223 Calories, 3g Total Carbs, 2g Net Carbs, 17g Total Fat, 15g Protein, 1g Sugar, 1g Fiber.

**Macros:** 28% Protein, 68% Fat, and 4% Carbs

## GARLIC CHICKEN PIECES

**Prep time: 10 minutes**

**Cook time: 10 minutes**

**Serve: 4**

**Ingredients:**

1 tablespoon of garlic minced)

1 egg

1-pound of roughly chopped chicken fillets

½ teaspoon of salt

3 tablespoons of almond milk

¼ teaspoon of olive oil

**Directions:**

- Beat and whisk the egg in a bowl.
- Add almond milk and minced garlic.
- Add oil and salt.
- Whisk until the mixture is homogenous.
- Add chopped chicken into egg mixture and ensure proper coating.
- Put chicken in the instant pot and close the instant pot.
- Set to poultry mode and adjust to high pressure.
- Allow cooking for 10minutes and quick release pressure.
- Chill and serve.

**Nutrition**: calories: 263, carbs: 1.4g, fiber: 0.3g, fat: 12.5g, protein: 34.6g

## CHICKEN PHO

**Prep time: 10minutes**

**Cook time: 15 minutes**

**Serve: 2**

**Ingredients:**

¼ teaspoon of coriander seeds

1 teaspoon of chopped ginger

1 clove of peeled garlic

¼ chopped apple

3 cups of water

1 tablespoon of stockfish

½ teaspoon of salt

2 chicken thighs

1 tablespoon of honey (raw)

½ zucchini

**Directions:**

- Cut the garlic cloves and put in the instant pot.
- Add chopped ginger and coriander seeds
- Pour water.
- Add salt and chopped apple.
- Add raw honey and fish stock.
- Cut the zucchini and add to the mixture.
- Add in the chicken thighs.
- With the aid of a wooden spoon, stir the mixture and close the instant pot.
- Select manual mode and adjust pressure to high.
- Allow cooking for 15 minutes and quick-release.
- Serve.

**Nutrition**: calories: 200, carbs: 9.5g, fiber: 1.4g, fat: 10.3g, protein: 20g

# SPICY TURKEY CUBES

**Prep time: 20 minutes**

**Cook time: 15 minutes**

**Serve: 2**

**Ingredients:**

14 oz. roughly chopped turkey fillet

1 teaspoon of black pepper (ground)

1 teaspoon of chili pepper

1 teaspoon of olive oil

1 chopped tomato

½ teaspoon of parsley (chopped)

1 teaspoon of cilantro

1 clove of chopped garlic

3 tablespoons of chicken stock

1 teaspoon of ghee

**Directions:**

- Combine black pepper, chili pepper, olive oil, chopped tomato, cilantro, chopped garlic and chopped parsley in the bowl.
- Using a hand blender, blend it.
- Combine spice mixture and chopped turkey fillet then stir gently.
- Add in chicken stock and gently stir.
- Allow marinating for 10 minutes.
- Put the ghee in the bowl contained in the instant pot set to sauté mode.

- Add in turkey and close the instant pot.
- Select poultry mode and adjust to high pressure.
- Allow cooking for 15 minutes and quick-release.
- Open the instant pot and serve.

**Nutrition**: calories: 307, carbs: 2.8g, fiber: 0.8g, fat: 2.1g, protein: 44.5g

## HONEY TURKEY BREAST

**Prep time: 10 minutes**

**Cook time: 25 minutes**

**Serve: 4**

**Ingredients:**

1-pound of turkey breast

1 tablespoon of salt

2 tablespoons of honey (raw)

½ teaspoon of black pepper (ground)

1 teaspoon of rosemary

½ cup of chicken stock

**Direction:**

- Combine rosemary, raw honey, salt, and ground pepper in bowl.
- Whisk until it becomes homogenous.
- Rub honey mixture on turkey breasts and allow for 10 minutes.
- Pour chicken stock into the instant pot and add in the turkey breast.
- Close the instant pot and set to poultry mode and adjust to high pressure.
- Allow cooking for 25 minutes and quick release.
- Transfer to serving plate and serve.

**Nutrition**: calories: 153, carbs: 13.9g, fiber: 0.8g, fat: 2g, protein: 19.5g

## PAPRIKA CHICKEN

**Prep time: 15 minutes**

**Cook time: 12 minutes**

**Serve: 4**

**Ingredients:**

1 red pepper (sweet)

1 tablespoon olive oil

1 tablespoon of smoked paprika

½ teaspoon of salt

1 tablespoon of chicken stock

1-pound of chicken thigh

**Directions:**

- Cut the sweet pepper.
- Combine olive oil and smoked paprika.
- Add salt and chicken stock.
- Stir mixture and then rub mixture on the chicken thigh.
- Add in the sweet pepper and allow marinate for 5 minutes.
- Pour 1 cup of water into the instant pot.
- Put in trivet and then place chicken thigh on it.
- Set to poultry mode and adjust to high pressure.
- Allow cooking for 12 minutes and release pressure naturally.
- Transfer to serving plates and serve.

**Nutrition**: calories: 260, carbs: 3.2g, fiber: 1.1g, fat: 12.2g, protein: 33.4g

# KETO CHICKEN THIGH

**Prep time: 10 minutes**

**Cook time: 11 minutes**

**Serve: 6**

**Ingredients:**

6 chicken thighs

1 teaspoon of cilantro

1 teaspoon of oregano

1 teaspoon of nutmeg

½ cup of water

½ teaspoon of garlic (minced)

**Directions:**

- Combine the cilantro, oregano, minced garlic and nutmeg in a shallow bowl.
- Stir well.
- Generously rub chicken thighs with mixture.
- Pour in ½ cup of water in bowl contained in the instant pot.
- Put in trivet and add in the chicken thighs.
- Set to poultry mode and adjust to high pressure.
- Allow cooking for 11 minutes and allow natural pressure release.
- Transfer chicken to serving plate and enjoy.

**Nutrition**: calories: 256, carbs: 0.4g, fiber: 0.2g, fat: 10g, protein: 38.6g

# CHICKEN SHAWARMA

**Prep time: 10 minutes**

**Cook time: 10 minutes**

**Serve: 4**

**Ingredients:**

1 pound of skinless, boneless chicken breast or thigh

3 tablespoons of Shawarma spice mix

3 teaspoons of olive oil

¼ cup of water

1 cup of onions (thinly sliced)

1 cup of Tzatziki Sauce

4 large lettuce leaves

**Directions:**

- Get a zip-top bag and put in the chicken thighs. Add Shawarma mix and olive oil and rub until the chicken is observed to be evenly coated.
- Put the chicken in the refrigerator for 24 hours to allow marinate.
- Select sauté mode on the instant pot and adjust to high pressure to allow preheating. When it is hot, add 2 teaspoons of olive oil and allow shimmering. In a single layer, add in chicken and allow smearing and then flip it. This should take a total of 4 minutes.
- Add onion and then add in water. Scrape up brown bits at the bottom of the pot.
- Close the instant pot and select manual. Adjust to high pressure and allow cooking for 10 minutes.
- Quick-release and open the instant pot.
- Wrap chicken with lettuce leave and serve with tzatziki sauce.

**Nutrition**: calories: 267, carbs: 4g, fiber: 1g, fat: 15g, protein: 28g

# CHICKEN TIKKA MASALA

**Prep time: 20 minutes**

**Cook time: 10 minutes**

**Serve: 6**

**FOR THE MARINADE**

4 cloves of minced garlic

½ cup of Greek yogurt

2 teaspoons of fresh ginger (minced)

½ teaspoon of cayenne

½ teaspoon of turmeric

1 teaspoon of paprika (smoked)

1 teaspoon of Garam Masala

1 teaspoon of salt

1 teaspoon of liquid smoke

½ teaspoon of ground cumin

1 ½ pound of skinless, boneless chicken thigh or breast

**FOR SAUCE**

1 chopped onion

1 chopped carrot

1 can of undrained diced tomatoes

2 teaspoons of minced fresh ginger

5 cloves of minced garlic

½ teaspoon of cayenne

1 teaspoon of ground turmeric

1 teaspoon of paprika (smoked)

2 teaspoons of Garam Masala

1 teaspoon of salt

1 teaspoon of ground cumin

**THE DISH**

1 teaspoon of Garam Masala

1 cup of full-fat coconut milk or heavy cream (whipping)

½ cup of fresh cilantro

**Directions:**

**MARINADE**

In a bowl, mix garlic, yogurt, turmeric, ginger, paprika, cayenne, cumin, salt, Garam Masala and liquid smoke. Add and stir chicken to coat and marinate for 2 hours in the refrigerator.

**SAUCE**

- In the bowl contained in the instant pot, mix tomatoes, onion, garlic, carrot, cayenne, turmeric, ginger, salt, paprika, garam masala and cumin. Place marinade chicken on top of sauce.
- Close the instant pot and set to manual mode. Adjust to high pressure and allow cooking for 10 minutes.
- Quick-release pressure and open the instant pot.
- Remove chicken and keep aside.
- Tilt toe bowl contained in the instant pot and puree the sauce with an immersion blender.

**DISH**

- To the sauce, add garam masala and cream and then stir.
- Take out half the sauce and freeze to be used later.
- Put removed chicken back to sauce and garnish using cilantro.
- Serve.

**Nutrition**: calories: 366, carbs: 8g, fiber: 2g, fat: 24g, protein: 29g

## MEXICAN STYLE CHICKEN WITH RED SALSA

**Prep time: 10 minutes**

**Cook time: 15 minutes**

**Serve: 8**

**Ingredients:**

2 pounds skinless, boneless chicken thigh

1 ½ tablespoons of chili powder

1 ½ tablespoons of cumin (ground)

2 tablespoons of vegetable oil

1 tablespoon of salt

1 can of tomato paste

1 can of undrained diced tomato

3 cloves of minced garlic

1 small chopped onion

½ cup of sour cream

2 ounces of jalapeno pickle with juice

**Directions:**

- Preheat the bowl contained in the instant pot by selecting sauté and set to high heat.
- Get a medium bowl and coat chicken with chili powder, salt and cumin.
- Put in oil in bowl contained in the instant pot and allow shimmering.
- Add in coated chicken and allow cooking for 5 minutes.
- Add in tomato paste, tomatoes, jalapeno, garlic and onion.
- Close the instant pot and set to manual mode. Set to high pressure and allow cooking for 15 minutes.
- Allow pressure release naturally and quick-release pressure.
- Shred chicken with the aid of fork and serve with sour cream topping.

**Nutrition**: calories: 329, carbs: 6g, fiber: 2g, fat: 24g, protein: 21g

## NOW AND LATER BUTTER CHICKEN

**Prep time: 15 minutes**

**Cook time: 10 minutes**

**Serve: 4**

**Ingredients:**

1 can of undrained diced tomatoes

1 tablespoon of fresh ginger (minced)

5 cloves of minced garlic

1 teaspoon of cayenne

1 teaspoon of turmeric (ground)

2 divided teaspoons of Garam Masala

1 teaspoon of smoked paprika

1 teaspoon of salt

1 teaspoon of cumin (ground)

½ cup of unsalted butter

1 pound of skinless, boneless chicken breast

½ cup of heavy cream (whipping)

4 cups of cauliflower rice

¼ cup of fresh cilantro

**Directions:**

- Put the garlic, tomatoes, turmeric, ginger, paprika, cayenne, cumin, 1 teaspoon of garam masala, salt and cumin. Mix and put chicken on sauce.
- Close the instant pot and set to manual mode. Set to high pressure and allow cooking for 10 minutes.
- Allow natural pressure release and remove chicken.
- Use an immersion blender to puree the sauce mixture until smooth and allow to cool before adding other ingredients.
- Add the cream, butter cubes, cilantro and remaining 1 teaspoon of garam masala. Stir well and you should observe the sauce is thick.
- Take out half of the sauce and freeze for later use.
- Shred the chicken and put back into the sauce.
- Preheat the bowl contained in the instant pot and set to sauté. Set to low heat. Allow chicken heat.
- Serve with cauliflower rice.

**Nutrition**: calories: 512, carbs: 10g, fiber: 6g, fat: 36g, protein: 31g

## DAN DAN-SYLE CHICKEN

**Prep time: 5 minutes**

**Cook time: 7 minutes**

**Serve:** 4

**Ingredients:**

2 tablespoons of peanut butter (creamy)

2 teaspoons of soy sauce

1 tablespoon of doubanjiang

1 teaspoon of red pepper flakes

2 teaspoons of rice wine vinegar

¼ cup of hot water

1 teaspoon of ground Sichuan peppercorns

¼ cup of water (room temp.)

1 pound of skinless, boneless chicken breast

1 tablespoon of sesame oil

1 package of rinsed shirataki noodles

¼ cup of fresh cilantro (chopped)

¼ cup of peanuts (chopped)

**Directions:**

- Get a medium bowl and mix the doubanjiang, peanut butter, vinegar, soy sauce, peppercorns, hot water and red pepper flakes.
- Place chicken in the bowl and coat with mixture. Allow marinating for 30 minutes.
- Put chicken and marinade in the bowl contained in the instant pot and pour in the water at room temperature.
- Close the instant pot and set to manual mode. Set pressure to high and allow cooking for 7 minutes.

- Allow natural release of pressure for 10 minutes and then quick-release.
- Separately, prepare noodles according to instruction and mix with the chicken when done.
- Stir in sesame oil and garnish with cilantro and peanuts if desired.

**Nutrition**: calories: 297, carbs: 5g, fiber: 5g, fat: 17g, protein: 26g

## SAVORY SHRIMP WITH TOMATOES AND FETA

**Prep time: 10 minutes**

**Cook time: 1 minute**

**Serve: 6**

**Ingredients:**

3 tablespoons of butter (unsalted)

½ teaspoon of red pepper flakes

1 tablespoon of garlic

1 can of undrained diced tomatoes

1 ½ cups of chopped onion

1 teaspoon of salt

1 teaspoon of dried oregano

1 cup of crumbled feta cheese

1 pound of peeled frozen shrimp

¼ cup of chopped parsley

½ cup of sliced black olives

**Directions:**

- Preheat the bowl contained in the instant pot by setting to sauté and setting to high heat. Add butter when heated and allow until foaming is observed. Add red pepper flakes and garlic and cook until 1 minute.
- Add tomato, salt, oregano and onion and stir.
- Add in frozen shrimp.
- Close the instant pot and select manual, setting to low pressure and allowing cooking or 1 minute. After cooking, quick-release pressure.
- Mix shrimp into the tomato broth.
- Allow cooling before serving and sprinkle olives, parsley and feta cheese. You can have this dish with mashed cauliflower if you desire.

**Nutrition**: calories: 361, carbs: 11g, fiber: 2g, fat: 22g, protein: 30g

## EASY LOBSTER BISQUE

**Prep time: 10 minutes**

**Cook time: 4 minutes**

**Serve: 4**

**Ingredients:**

1 chopped onion

2 teaspoons of ghee

1 tablespoon of garlic (minced)

2 cups of chicken broth

1 tablespoon of fresh ginger (minced)

3 cups of cauliflower (chopped)

1 cup of tomatoes (chopped)

½ teaspoon of salt

2 tablespoons of ready-made pesto

1 pound of cooked lobster meat

2 teaspoons of black pepper (freshly ground)

1 cup of heavy cream (whipping)

**Directions:**

- Preheat the bowl contained in the instant pot by setting to sauté mod and high heat. Add in ghee and allow to heat and is shimmering. Add in garlic, onion, and ginger. Allow to sauté for 3 minutes or till it is softened.
- Pour chicken broth in and stir. Add in cauliflower, salt, tomatoes, pepper and pesto.
- Close the instant pot and set to manual mode. Adjust to high pressure and allow cooking for 4 minutes.
- Allow natural pressure release for 10minutes and quick-release.
- Tilt the pot and puree the vegetables using and immersion blender. Do this until the pot is smooth.
- Set the instant pot to sauté mode and set to high heat. Add in the lobster and allow to heat through. Stir in cream and serve.

**Nutrition**: calories: 441, carbs: 10g, fiber: 4g, fat: 30g, protein: 30g

## CREAMY SHRIMP SCAMPI

**Prep time: 5 minutes**

**Cook time: 2 minutes**

**Serve: 6**

**Ingredients:**

2 tablespoons of butter (unsalted)

½ teaspoon of smoked paprika

4 cloves of minced garlic

1 pound of peeled shrimp (frozen)

¼ teaspoon of red pepper flakes

½ teaspoon of salt

½ cup of chicken broth or water

1 teaspoon of black pepper (freshly ground)

½ cup of parmesan cheese

½ cup of heavy cream (heavy)

2 cups of zucchini noodles (cooked)

**Directions:**

- Preheat the bowl contained in the instant pot by setting to sauté and high heat. When heated, add in butter and heat till foaming is observed. Add red pepper flakes and garlic and then sauté until the garlic is observed to be browned slightly. This should be in 2 minutes.
- Add in the paprika followed by the zucchini noodles, frozen shrimp, pepper and salt.
- Pour in broth or water and add ½ teaspoon of salt if you are using water.
- Close the instant pot and set to manual mode, set to high pressure. Allow cooking for 2 minutes and quick-pressure release. Open the instant pot.
- Set the instant pot to sauté and set to high heat. Add in cheese and cream and continue stirring until it melts. This should take about a minute.
- Share the zucchini noodles to serving bowls and top with creamy shrimp scampy.
- Serve.

**Nutrition:** Calories: 332, carbs: 4g, fiber: 0g, fat: 23g, protein: 28g

## CHINESE-STYLE STEAMED GINGER SCALLION FISH
**Prep time: 10 minutes**

**Cook time:** 2 minutes

**Serve:** 4

**Ingredients:**

1 pound of tilapia fillets

2 tablespoons of rice wine

3 tablespoons of soy sauce

1 teaspoon of fresh ginger (minced)

1 tablespoon of doubanjiang

3 tablespoons of peanut oil

1 teaspoon of garlic (minced)

¼ cup of julienned scallions

2 tablespoons of julienned fresh ginger

¼ cup of fresh cilantro (chopped)

**Directions:**

- Put fish fillets in a shallow bowl. Get a small bowl and mix the rice wine, soy sauce, minced ginger, doubanjiang and garlic. Pour mixture over the fish and allow marinate for 30 minutes.
- Remove fish from marinade and put into a steamer basket. Make sure to reserve the marinade.
- Pour in 2 cups of water to bowl contained in the instant pot. Place over the water, the steamer basket and close the instant pot. Set to manual mode and set to low pressure. Allow cooking for 2 minutes and quick-release pressure. Open the instant pot.
- While fish is cooking, get a sauce-pan and place on medium heat and add in oil. Allow shimmering and add in julienned ginger. Sauté for 10 seconds. Add in cilantro, scallions and stir while frying for up to 2 minutes. And add

the marinade initially reserved and allow boil vigorously till cooked through.
- Share fish in serving plates and top with sauce. Serve and enjoy.

**Nutrition**: calories: 185, carbs: 2g, fiber: 0g, fat: 10g protein: 24g

# SESAME-GINGER CHICKEN

**Prep time: 5 minutes**

**Cook time: 10 minutes**

**Serve: 6**

**Ingredients:**

1 ½ pounds of skinless, boneless chicken thighs

1 tablespoon of sesame oil

2 tablespoons of soy sauce

1 tablespoon of garlic (minced)

1 tablespoon of fresh ginger (minced)

1 tablespoon of rice vinegar

1 tablespoon of Truvia

**Directions:**

- Place chicken inside heatproof bowl and add sesame oil, soy sauce, garlic, ginger, vinegar and Truvia. Coat the chicken while stirring and use and aluminum foil to cover the bowl.
- To the bowl contained in the instant pot, add 2 cups of water and put trivet in. place the bowl on trivet and close the instant pot.
- Set to manual mode and set to high pressure. Allow cooking for 10 minutes and quick-release. Open the instant pot.

- Take out chicken and shred to desire and put back into the liquid contained in the bowl.
- Serve with salad or zoodles.

**Nutrition**: calories: 272, carbs: 4g, fiber: 0g, fat: 20g, protein: 19g

## CHICKEN BRATWURST MEATBALLS WITH CABBAGE

**Prep time: 15 minutes**

**Cook time: 4 minutes**

**Serve: 4**

**Ingredients:**

1 pound of chicken (ground)

2 divided teaspoons of salt

¼ cup of heavy cream (whipping)

1 ½ teaspoons of black pepper (freshly ground)

½ teaspoon of ground allspice

½ cup of milk

5 cups of green cabbage (thickly chopped)

2 tablespoons of butter (unsalted)

½ teaspoon of caraway seed (ground)

**Directions:**

- To prepare meatballs, put chicken in bowl and add 1 teaspoon of salt, cream, allspice, caraway and ½ teaspoon of pepper. Make sure to thoroughly mix and refrigerate for 30 minutes.

- Scoop and mold medium-sized meatballs and put half of them in the bowl contained in the instant pot and cover with half of the cabbage. Now put the remaining meatballs on the cabbage and top the meatballs with remaining cabbage.
- Place some of the butter, pour in milk and sprinkle with 1 teaspoon of pepper and 1 teaspoon of salt.
- Close the instant pot and set to manual mode. Set to high pressure and allow cooking for 4 minutes.
- Quick-release pressure and open the instant pot.
- Serve and enjoy.

**Nutrition**: calories: 338, carbs: 7g, fiber: 3g, fat: 23g, protein: 23g

## HOMEMADE SLICED TURKEY AND GRAVY

Paired with Cheesecake and Cauliflower Puree, this is the perfect keto-dish for festivities.

**Serves: 8**

**Time for Preparation: 10 minutes**

**Time for Pressure Cooking: 20 minutes on High**

**Release: Natural**

**Sauté: 20 minutes**

**Total Time: 1 hour and 15 minutes**

**Gluten-free and Nut-free**

**Ingredients:**

½ teaspoon of ground nutmeg

½ teaspoon of freshly ground black pepper

1 tablespoon of Ghee

1 teaspoon of sea salt

1 tablespoon of dried sage

1 tablespoon of dried thyme

1 tablespoon of crushed garlic

1 teaspoon of ground marjoram

1 onion, quartered 1 celery stalk, chopped

1 to 2 tablespoons of grass-fed beef gelatin or ¼ to ½ teaspoon of xanthan gum

3 cups of Bone Broth or chicken broth, divided

3½ pounds of bone-in, skin-on turkey breast

**Preparation:**

- Mix the garlic, salt, thyme, nutmeg, sage, marjoram, and pepper. Spread the mixture of spices on every part of the turkey breast.
- Get the pressure cooker and put in it 2 cups of bone broth, celery and onion. Place the trivet in it, then keep the turkey breast on it, with its skin-side up.
- Lock the lid properly and set the steam release knob to seal. Set pressure to High and time to 20 minutes. Naturally release the pressure after cooking. Unlock the lid and remove it. Check the internal temperature of the turkey with the help of a kitchen thermometer. Lock the lid and allow to cook for 5 to 7 minutes more if the turkey isn't at 165oF. More so, the thermometer should not be lower than 165oF.
- Get the turkey breast out of the pressure cooker and place on a serving platter. Use the foil to tent so it remains warm.
- Use a metal strainer to separate the solids from the drippings of the turkey. Put the drippings back into the pressure cooker, but get rid of the solids.
- Pick the Sauté or Browning feature on the pressure cooker then set on low heat. Pour in the 1 cup of bone broth left, then let the broth and drippings to simmer for 20 minutes. Add any thickener you prefer when the time is almost complete. Mix 1 tablespoon of gelatin into 4 to 5 tablespoons of cold water and allow to sit for a minute, if you choose to use beef gelatin. Add the gravy then mix properly so it dissolves completely. Add the remaining gelatin along with 4 to 5 tablespoons of water then mix until it gets to a consistency you like. The gelatin is sure to thicken as it cools. If however, you decide to use xanthan gum instead, stir in ¼ teaspoon of it at a time till the gravy gets to the consistency you prefer.

- Mix the ghee into the gravy then use pepper and salt to season. Allow to cool a bit before you serve.
- Carve the turkey breast and serve it smothered in gravy.

**Per Serving Contains:** 733 Calories, 2g Total Carbs, 3g Net Carbs, 59g Total Fat, 46g Protein, 1g Sugar, 0g Fiber.

**Macros:** 26% Protein, 73% Fat, and 1% Carbs

## CHICKEN KORMA

This korma dish is made up of a lot of ingredients that combine to form a delicious curry sauce.

**Serves:** 6

**Time for Preparation:** 8 minutes

**Sauté:** 3 minutes

**Time for Pressure Cooking:** 10 minutes on High pressure

**Release:** Quick

**Simmer:** 15 minutes

**Total Time:** 46 minutes

**Dairy-free and Gluten-free**

**Ingredients:**

¼ to ½ teaspoon of red pepper flakes

¼ cup of chopped fresh cilantro

¼ teaspoon of cayenne pepper

¼ teaspoon of freshly ground black pepper

½ cup of almond flour

½ teaspoon of ground cloves

½ teaspoon of ground turmeric

½ teaspoon of ground nutmeg

½ cup of grated unsweetened coconut

1 teaspoon of sea salt

1 large sliced yellow onion

1 teaspoon of fennel seeds

1 teaspoon of ground cumin

1 teaspoon of ground cinnamon

1 (13.5-ounce) can of unsweetened coconut milk

2 teaspoons of ground coriander

2 tablespoons of divided garam masala

2 tablespoons of minced peeled fresh ginger

2 pounds of frozen boneless, skinless chicken thighs

3 large diced tomatoes

3 tablespoons of coconut oil

4 minced garlic cloves

**Preparation**

- Choose the Sauté or Browning feature on the pressure cooker then set on medium heat. Heat the coconut oil in the cooker until it shimmers before adding the garlic, ginger, and onion. Sauté for about 2 or 3 minutes.
- Add the red pepper flakes, coriander, turmeric, tomatoes, cinnamon, nutmeg, black pepper, ½ cup of water, coconut milk, 1 tablespoon of garam masala, cumin, cayenne pepper, fennel, cloves, salt, and frozen chicken thighs. Stir until it is well mixed.
- Lock the lid properly and set the steam release knob to seal. Set to high pressure and adjust time to 10 minutes. Quick release the pressure after cooking. Unlock the lid and remove it.
- Use a slotted spoon to remove the chicken from the pot and place in a plate. Shred the meat into small pieces then set it aside.
- Blend the sauce with an immersion blender until it becomes smooth. Alternatively, you may put the sauce in a blender and blend till it is smooth before transferring back to the pressure cooker.

- Add the grated coconut, the 1 tablespoon of garam masala left, and the almond flour to the sauce. Choose Sauté or Brown and allow to simmer for 15 minutes or as soon as it reduces by half.
- Place the chicken back into the pressure cooker and mix it properly with the sauce. Serve along with the chopped cilantro.

**Per Serving Contains:** 465 Calories, 12g Total Carbs, 9g Net Carbs, 39g Total Fat, 23g Protein, 5g Sugar, 3g Fiber.

**Macros:** 18% Protein, 73% Fat, and 9% Carbs

## MOLE CHICKEN

This delicious dish is derived from the traditional Mexican dish. It goes well with Dairy-Free Sour Cream and Coconut-Lime Cauliflower Rice.

**Serves:** 6

**Time for Preparation:** 5 minutes

**Sauté:** 10 minutes

**Time for Pressure Cooking:** 15 minutes on High pressure

**Release:** Quick

**Total Time:** 40 minutes

**Dairy-free and Gluten-free**

**Ingredients:**

¼ cup of fresh chopped cilantro

⅓ cup of creamy peanut butter

½ teaspoon of ground cloves

1 minced onion

1 minced red bell pepper

1 teaspoon of adobo sauce

1 teaspoon of ground cumin

1 teaspoon of ground cinnamon

1 chipotle chile in adobo sauce, diced

1 (14.5-ounce) can of diced tomatoes with their juices

1½ tablespoons of chili powder

2 avocados, halved, pitted, peeled, and diced

2 pounds of boneless, skinless chicken thighs

3 tablespoons of coconut oil

3 tablespoons of cocoa powder

5 minced garlic cloves

6 to 8 drops liquid stevia or preferred powdered sugar substitute equivalent to 1 to 2

tablespoons sugar (optional)

**Preparation:**

- Sauté or brown the pressure cooker and set on medium heat before heating the coconut oil till it shimmers. Add the garlic and onions and Sauté for about 1 or 2 minutes until they become fragrant. Stir the diced tomatoes as well as their juices in, add ½ cup of water, then scrape the browned bits at the bottom of the pot. Put in the chicken.
- Lock the lid properly and seal the steam release knob. Set on high pressure and adjust time to 15 minutes. Quick release the pressure after cooking. Unlock the lid and remove it.
- Move the chicken to a bowl or a work surface then use 2 forks to shred the meat. Set it aside.
- Choose the Sauté or browning on the pressure cooker again then add the peanut butter, cocoa powder, chipotle chile, cinnamon, bell pepper, chili powder, cumin, adobo sauce, and cloves. Sauté until the sauce reduces about half way, this should last for about 5 to 8 minutes.
- Blend with an immersion blender, or use a stand blender till it gets really smooth. Use the stevia if you choose to.
- Pour the sauce on the chicken and mix really well. Garnish with the chopped cilantro and diced avocado before you serve.

**Per Serving Contains:** 451 Calories, 18g Total Carbs, 10g Net Carbs, 29g Total Fat, 35g Protein, 8g Sugar, 8g Fiber.

**Macros:** 30% Protein, 55% Fat, and 15% Carbs

## BUTTER CHICKEN

This dish, which takes about 30 minutes to prepare, is rich in cream and Indian spices.

**Serves:** 6

**Time for Preparation:** 5 minutes

**Sauté:** 5 minutes

**Time for Pressure Cooking:** 3 minutes on high pressure

**Release:** 10 minutes natural, then Quick

**Total Time:** 33 minutes

**Gluten-free and Nut-free**

**Ingredients:**

¼ cup of chopped fresh cilantro

½ teaspoon of cayenne pepper

1 teaspoon of sea salt

1 teaspoon of ground turmeric

1 tablespoon of garam masala

1 tablespoon of smoked paprika

1 tablespoon of ground coriander

1 cup of full-fat coconut cream or heavy cream

1 (14.5-ounce) can of diced tomatoes with their juices

1 tablespoon of grass-fed beef gelatin or ¼ teaspoon xanthan gum (optional)

2 teaspoons of ground cumin

2 tablespoons of minced peeled fresh ginger

2 pounds of boneless, skinless chicken thighs, cut into 2-inch cubes

5 tablespoons of unsalted grass-fed butter

6 minced garlic cloves

**Preparation:**

- Choose Sauté or browning on the pressure cooker then set to medium heat. Put the butter in the cooker to melt until it foams. Add the garlic and ginger then Sauté until it becomes aromatic.
- Add the cumin, the diced tomatoes and their juices, garam masala, smoked paprika, cayenne, cumin, coriander, turmeric, and salt. Cook for about 3 to 5 minutes while gently stirring. Put in the chicken then mix until the sauce coats it fully.
- Lock the lid securely then seal the steam release knob. Adjust pressure level to High and time to 3 minutes. Naturally release the pressure for 10 minutes after cooking, then quick release any pressure left. Unlock the lid and remove it.
- Use a slotted spoon to get out the chicken then set it aside. The sauce should be poured into the blender to finely puree.
- Choose Sauté or browning on the pressure cooker again, then return the sauce to the cooker. Add the chicken and coconut cream, then mix properly.
- Get a small bowl and put in it a tablespoon of gelatin (optional) then add 4 to 5 tablespoons of cold water. Allow to sit for a minute before adding ¼ of the gelatin mixture and butter chicken. Mix until it dissolves. Keep adding the gelatin until the sauce gets to the desired consistency (though the gelatin will thicken as it cools). Use the cilantro to garnish the butter chicken. Serve.

**Per Serving Contains:** 409 Calories, 7g Total Carbs, 5g Net Carbs, 27g Total Fat, 32g Protein, 2g Sugar, 2g Fiber.

**Macros:** 32% Protein, 61% Fat, and 7% Carbs

## CHICKEN CACCIATORE

This dish is made easier with a pressure cooker. To get a thicker sauce, Sauté right after the pressure cooking has been completed.

**Serves:** 6

**Time for Preparation:** 10 minutes

**Sauté:** 9 minutes

**Time for Pressure Cook:** 10 minutes in high pressure

**Release:** Quick

**Total Time:** 39 minutes

**Gluten-free and Nut-free**

**Ingredients:**

¼ to ½ teaspoon of red pepper flakes

¼ teaspoon of freshly ground black pepper, with additional for seasoning

½ cup of dry white wine

½ cup of pitted black olives

½ cup of chopped fresh basil

½ cup of grated Parmesan cheese

½ pounds of bone-in, skin-on chicken thighs

1 diced onion

1 diced red bell pepper

1 teaspoon of dried thyme

1 teaspoon of onion powder

1 teaspoon of dried oregano

1 teaspoon of dried rosemary

1 teaspoon of sea salt, plus more for seasoning

1 (14.5-ounce) can of diced tomatoes with their juices

3 tablespoons of Ghee

5 minced garlic cloves

**Preparation:**

- Season both sides of the chicken with a teaspoon of salt and one-quarter teaspoon of pepper. Choose Sauté or Browning on the pressure cooker then set heat to medium. Melt the ghee inside the cooker till it shimmers. Add the chicken thighs with their skin facing downwards, cook until it turns a golden brown for about 4 to 5 minutes. Flip then cook each side for 1 to 2 minutes. Take the chicken thighs out and place them on a place before setting aside.
- Put in the garlic, bell pepper, and onion, then Sauté for a minute or 2 while stirring. Add the wine, the tomatoes with their juices, onion powder, red pepper flakes, oregano, rosemary, and thyme. Use pepper and salt for seasoning. Stir well with a wooden spoon while scraping the brown bits stuck to the pot's bottom. Put the chicken thighs back into the pressure cooker.
- Lock the lid properly then seal using the steam release knob. Set on high pressure then set time to 10 minutes. Quick release the pressure after cooking, before unlocking and removing the lid. Move the chicken thighs to a plate before setting aside.
- Choose Sauté or Browning again to make the sauce simmer. Add the basil as well as the olives and simmer until the sauce reduces to your preferred consistency.
- Put the chicken thighs back into the pressure cooker and use Parmesan cheese as topping. Season using pepper and salt. Serve.

**Pairing Tip:** Pairing this dish with Zucchini Noodles or Spaghetti Squash will change the macros to the following: 19% protein, 72% fat, and 9% carbs.

**Per Serving Contains:** 419 Calories, 10g Total Carbs, 7g Net Carbs, 30g Total Fat, 22g Protein, 6g Sugar, 3g Fiber.

**Macros:** 22% Protein, 68% Fat, and 10% Carbs

## CHICKEN BUFFALO MEATBALLS

**Serves:** 4

**Time for Preparation:** 5 minutes

**Sauté:** 8 minutes

**Time for Pressure Cooking:** 5 minutes on high pressure

**Release:** Natural

**Total Time:** 43 minutes

**Gluten-free**

**Ingredients:**

¼ teaspoon of freshly ground black pepper

½ cup of almond flour

½ teaspoon of sea salt

1 large egg

1 pound of ground chicken

1 teaspoon of garlic powder

1 teaspoon of onion powder

1 recipe of Avocado Ranch Dressing

1¼ cups of hot sauce with no added sugars, like Frank's RedHot, divided

2 scallions, green parts only, sliced

2 tablespoons of unsalted grass-fed butter

**Preparation:**

- Put the ground chicken, almond flour, egg, ¼ cup of hot sauce, onion powder, pepper, garlic powder, and salt together in a large bowl. Mix the ingredients properly until they are well combined.
- Scoop the 1-inch balls out of the meat mixture with the use of your hands or a small ice cream scoop.
- Choose Sauté or Browning on the pressure cooker then set heat to high. Melt the butter until it shimmers. Put the meatballs in small batches into the pressure cooker. Take 1 to 2 minutes for each batch to brown all sides evenly. Repeat the process until all the meatballs are lightly browned before moving to a plate.
- Scrape up the bits stuck to the pan's bottom as soon as the meatballs are browned. Put the meatballs back into the pressure cooker then pour the 1 cup of hot sauce left on them.
- Lock the lid properly then set the steam release knob to seal. Set to high pressure and adjust time to 5 minutes. Naturally release the pressure after

cooking before unlocking and removing the lid. Take out the meatballs and put them on a platter. Top with the sliced scallion greens, use the ranch dressing as dipping. Serve.

**Per Serving Contains:** 420 Calories, 10g Total Carbs, 6g Net Carbs, 33g Total Fat, 25g Protein, 3g Sugar, 4g Fiber.

**Macros:** 24% Protein, 67% Fat, and 9% Carbs

## BARBECUE CHICKEN WINGS

**Serves: 6**

**Time for Preparation: 5 minutes**

**Time for Pressure Cooking: 5 minutes on High pressure**

**Release: Natural**

**Broil: 10 minutes**

**Total Time: 40 minutes**

**Gluten-free and Nut-free**

**Ingredient:**

½ cup of unsalted grass-fed butter, melted

½ cup of Sugar-Free Barbecue Sauce

1½ teaspoon of sea salt

2 pounds of split chicken wings

**Preparation:**

- Get a pressure cooker and pour ¾ cup of water into it. Place the trivet into the cooker then arrange the chicken wings on it.
- Lock the lid properly and set the steam release knob to seal. Set the pressure to High and time to 5 minutes. Naturally release the pressure after cooking.
- Mix the barbecue sauce, salt, and butter together in a small bowl while the pressure is being released.
- Preheat the oven and allow to broil.

- Unlock the lid and remove it when the pressure is done releasing. Get the wings out of the pressure cooker then move to a baking sheet very carefully. Brush the wings very well with sauce and broil for 5 minutes. Get the wings out of the oven, flip them over, coat with sauce, and broil for 5 more minutes, till the wings become crisp.
- Get the wings out of the oven and put the remaining sauce in it.

**Per Serving Contains**: 474 Calories, 2g Total Carbs, 2g Net Carbs, 40g Total Fat, 26g Protein, 0g Sugar, 0g Fiber.

**Macros:** 22% Protein, 76% Fat, and 2% Carbs

## CREAMY ARTICHOKE CHICKEN

Best paired with Zucchini Noodles or Spaghetti Squash, this recipe tastes great, especially due to the rich and creamy flavor the coconut cream brings.

**Serves: 6**

**Time for Preparation: 8 minutes**

**Sauté: 3 minutes**

**Time for Pressure Cooking: 13 minutes on High pressure**

**Release: Quick**

**Total Time: 31 minutes**

**Dairy-free, Gluten-free, and nut-free**

**Ingredients:**

¼ to ½ teaspoon of red pepper flakes

¼ teaspoon of freshly ground black pepper

½ cup of chopped fresh basil

½ cup of Avocado Oil Mayonnaise

½ cup of Bone Broth or chicken broth

1 chopped onion

1 teaspoon of sea salt

1 cup of full-fat coconut cream

1 tablespoon of onion powder

1 teaspoon of finely grated lemon zest

1 tablespoon of freshly squeezed lemon juice

1 (14-ounce) can of chopped artichoke hearts, drained

2 pounds of boneless, skinless chicken thighs

3 tablespoons of avocado oil

4 cups of fresh spinach

5 minced garlic cloves

**Preparation:**

- Choose Sauté or Browning on the pressure cooker then set heat on medium. Heat the avocado oil until it shimmers before adding the garlic and onion. Sauté for 2 to 3 minutes and make sure the onion is translucent.
- Add the lemon juice, broth, red pepper flakes, pepper, chicken, onion powder, and pepper.
- Lock the lid securely then adjust the steam release knob to seal. Set on High pressure and adjust time to 13 minutes. Quick release the pressure after cooking. Unlock the lid and remove it.
- Move the chicken to a medium-sized bowl, then use two forks to cut the meat into small pieces. Set it aside.
- Choose Sauté or Browning on the pressure cooker again. Add the spinach, coconut cream, lemon zest, chopped artichoke hearts, basil, and mayonnaise. Mix these ingredients properly then cook until the sauce starts thickening. Return the chicken to the pressure cooker then stir until it heats through.

.**Ingredient Substitution:** You can use cream cheese and also top with shredded Parmesan if you are not avoiding dairy.

**Per Serving Contains:** 504 Calories, 12g Total Carbs, 9g Net Carbs, 35g Total Fat, 35g Protein, 3g Sugar, 3g Fiber.

**Macros:** 28% Protein, 62% Fat, and 10% Carbs

# CHICKEN SHAWARMA

**Serves:** 6

**Time for Preparation:** 5 minutes, with additional 2 hours to marinate

**Sauté:** 4 minutes

**Time for Pressure Cooking:** 6 minutes on high pressure

**Release:** Quick

**Total Time:** 2 hours, 27 minutes

**Gluten-free and Nut-free**

**Ingredients:**

¼ cup of freshly squeezed lemon juice, plus 2 tablespoons

½ cup of tahini

½ teaspoon of ground cumin

½ teaspoon of ground allspice

½ teaspoon of smoked paprika

½ cup of crumbled feta cheese

½ teaspoon of red pepper flakes

½ teaspoon of ground cinnamon

½ cup of full-fat plain Greek yogurt

1 tablespoon of avocado oil

1 teaspoon of dried oregano

1 teaspoon of ground cardamom

2 teaspoons of chopped fresh parsley

2 pounds of boneless, skinless chicken thighs, cut into pieces

2½ teaspoons of sea salt, divided

3 cups of baby spinach

3 tablespoons of extra-virgin olive oil

4 garlic cloves, minced, plus 2 garlic cloves, peeled

Freshly ground black pepper

**Preparation:**

- Get a resealable bag and place your chicken in it. Add the minced garlic, avocado oil, cumin, red pepper flakes, cardamom, allspice, ¼ cup of lemon juice, yogurt, smoked paprika, oregano, cinnamon, and 2 teaspoons of salt. Seal the bag and shake well to properly spice up the chicken. Put in the refrigerator for 2 hours to marinate.
- Choose Sauté or Browning on the pressure cooker and set heat on medium. Put the chicken in the cooker then sear each side for a minute or two. Add marinade along with ½ cup of water.
- Lock the lid properly and seal the steam release knob. Adjust the pressure to high and time to 6 minutes.
- Meanwhile, combine the olive oil, the 2 tablespoons of lemon juice left, tahini, 2 whole peeled garlic cloves, the ½ teaspoon of salt left, and the parsley inside the food processor. Season this with pepper and process until it is consistently smooth.
- Quick release the pressure after cooking the chicken. Unlock the lid and remove it. Prepare a bed of fresh spinach in a serving plate and place the chicken on it. Evenly top with the feta and garlic sauce. Serve.

**Cooking Tip:** If you prefer your chicken shawarma crispy, firstly cook the chicken in the pressure cooker. Then heat a tablespoon or 2 of oil inside a pan and allow the chicken Sauté in it until the edges begin to get crispy.

**Per Serving Contains:** 482 Calories, 8g Total Carbs, 4g Net Carbs, 37g Total Fat, 33g Protein, 3g Sugar, 4g Fiber.

**Macros:** 27% Protein, 67% Fat, and 6% Carbs

## CASHEW CHICKEN

This Chinese-American dish is often made using soy sauce and brown sugar. However, in this recipe, the brown sugar has been totally eliminated, and the soy sauce replaced with coconut aminos. This is to reduce sugar content and create a healthier variation of the meal.

**Serves:** 4

**Time for Preparation:** 5 minutes

**Sauté:** 2 minutes

**Time for Pressure Cooking:** 5 minutes on high, with additional 0 minutes on high

**Release:** Quick

**Total Time:** 25 minutes

**Dairy-free and Gluten-free**

**Ingredients:**

Sea salt

¼ teaspoon of red pepper flakes

½ cup of coconut aminos

1 cup of toasted cashews

1 diced green bell pepper

1 tablespoon of sesame oil, for garnish

1 tablespoon of minced peeled fresh ginger

1 to 2 tablespoons of grass-fed beef gelatin or ¼ to 1 teaspoon of xanthan gum

1½ pounds of boneless, skinless chicken thighs, cut into 1-inch pieces

2 minced garlic cloves

2 tablespoons of fish sauce

2 tablespoons of coconut oil

2 tablespoons of apple cider vinegar

2 tablespoons of sesame seeds, for garnish

4 cups of chopped broccoli florets

Freshly ground black pepper

Sliced scallion greens, for garnish

**Preparation:**

- Choose Sauté or Browning on the pressure cooker and set on high heat. Let the coconut oil heat in it until it shimmers, then add the chicken and allow to brown lightly for a minute or 2.
- Meanwhile, get a small bowl and whisk in it the apple cider vinegar, garlic, red pepper flakes, coconut aminos, fish sauce, and ginger. Pour this sauce on the chicken when it is slightly browned.
- Lock the lid properly and seal. Set pressure to High and time to 5 minutes. Quick release the pressure after cooking. Unlock the lid and remove it.
- Stir in the broccoli and bell pepper. Relock the lid and seal then set time to 0 minutes. Quick release the pressure after cooking. Unlock the lid and remove it.
- Get a small bowl and mix in it 4 to 5 tablespoons of cold water and 1 tablespoon of gelatin then allow It sit for a minute. Add half of the gelatin mixture to the chicken then mix until it dissolves. Keep adding the gelatin until the sauce is as thick as you like it (note that the gelatin will keep thickening as it cools). Repeat the process with more gelatin and water as required. Stir for a minute or 2 till the sauce thickens.
- Add the cashews and mix well, before adding salt and pepper for seasoning. Garnish with the sliced scallion greens and sesame seeds, then drizzle with sesame oil.

**Per Serving Contains:** 419 Calories, 15g Total Carbs, 12g Net Carbs, 25g Total Fat, 33g Protein, 6g Sugar, 3g Fiber.

**Macros:** 32% Protein, 54% Fat, and 14% Carbs

## WHOLE CHICKEN

This clean meal is made easier to prepare using the pressure cooker. The ingredients are all natural – chicken, garlic, spices, and avocado oil.

**Serves:** 4

**Time for Preparation:** 10 minutes

**Sauté:** 8 minutes

**Time for Pressure Cooking:** 24 – 28 minutes on High pressure

**Release:** Natural

**Total Time:** 1 hour, 10 minutes

**Dairy-free, Nut-free, and Gluten-free**

**Ingredients:**

½ onion, cut into quarters

½ cup of chicken broth or water

½ teaspoon of cayenne pepper

1 halved lemon

1 teaspoon of dried thyme

1 teaspoon of garlic powder

1 (3- to 4-pound) whole chicken

1 teaspoon of freshly ground black pepper

2 teaspoons of paprika

2 tablespoons of avocado oil, divided

4 teaspoons of sea salt

6 crushed garlic cloves

**Preparation:**

- Get the giblets out of the chicken. Put the garlic, lemon halves, and onion quarters into the chicken's cavity. Tie the legs closed with a butcher's twine.
- Get a small bowl and mix the salt, thyme, garlic powder, cayenne pepper, paprika, black pepper, and garlic powder together. Apply a tablespoon of avocado oil and spice mixture on it.
- Choose Sauté or Browning on the pressure cooker and set to medium heat. Add the 1 tablespoon of avocado oil left and heat until it shimmers. Put the chicken in the cooker then brown for about 4 minutes. Flip it then brown the other side for about 3 to 4 minutes.

- Briefly get the chicken out of the pressure cooker so you can place the trivet inside. Keep the chicken breast on the trivet with its side up. Pour this in the broth. Lock the lid securely and seal the steam release knob. Set pressure to High and time to 24 to 28 minutes (although the cooking time depends on the chicken size; each round should be set on about 8 minutes per round).
- Naturally release the pressure after cooking. Unlock the lid and remove it.
- Get the chicken out of the pressure cooper then allow it rest for about 5 to 10 minutes before you serve.

**Leftover Tip:** Save the carcass so you can make bone broth with it.

**Per Serving Contains:** 295 Calories, 4g Total Carbs, 3g Net Carbs, 23g Total Fat, 18g Protein, 1g Sugar, 1g Fiber.

**Macros:** 25% Protein, 70% Fat, and 5% Carbs

## CREAMY SALSA VERDE CHICKEN

This nutrient-rich meal is very easy to prepare and will go well with lettuce wraps or salads. The addition of avocado and spinach makes this meal well-balanced enough to be eaten by itself.

**Serves:** 5

**Time for Preparation:** 5 minutes

**Sauté:** 3 minutes

**Time for Pressure Cooking:** 10 minutes on high pressure

**Release:** Quick

**Total Time:** 28 minutes

**Gluten-free and Nut-free**

**Ingredients:**

¼ cup of chopped fresh cilantro

½ cup of cream cheese

½ teaspoon of freshly ground black pepper

1 tablespoon of Ghee

1 teaspoon of sea salt

1 teaspoon of ground cumin

1 minced jalapeño pepper

1 (16-ounce) jar of salsa verde

1 avocado, halved, pitted, peeled, and chopped

2 cups of chopped spinach

2 pounds of boneless, skinless chicken thighs

4 minced garlic cloves

**Preparation:**

- Choose Sauté or Browning on the pressure cooker then set on medium heat. Let the ghee heat until it shimmers. Add the garlic then allow to Sauté for about a minute or 2 until it gets fragrant.
- Add the chicken thighs, salt, jalapeno, salsa verde, cumin, and pepper.
- Lock the lid and seal the steam release knob. Set pressure on High and time on 10 minutes. Quick release the pressure after cooking. Unlock the lid and remove it.
- Move the chicken thighs to a medium bowl then use 2 forks to shred the meat.
- Add the cream cheese, avocado, and chopped spinach to the juices left in the pressure cooker. Stir this until the spinach starts wilting. Add the shredded chicken then stir. Use the chopped cilantro to garnish before serving.

**Ingredient Substitution:** If you are dairy-free, use coconut cream instead of cream cheese.

**Per Serving Contains:** 399 Calories, 9g Total Carbs, 7g Net Carbs, 26.6g Total Fat, 31g Protein, 5g Sugar, 2g Fiber.

**Macros:** 32% Protein, 60% Fat, and 8% Carbs

# BEEF AND PORK

# KIELBASA AND SAUERKRAUT

**Serves: 6**

**Time for Preparation: 5 minutes**

**Sauté: 10 minutes**

**Pressure Cooking: 5 minutes on high pressure**

**Release: Quick**

**Total Time: 30 minutes**

**Gluten-free and Nut-free**

**Ingredients:**

⅓ cup of dry white wine

½ teaspoon of dried sage

½ apple, peeled and grated

½ cup of bone broth or chicken broth

½ teaspoon of freshly ground black pepper

1 sliced yellow onion

1 teaspoon of sea salt

1 teaspoon of dried thyme

1 (16-ounce) jar of sauerkraut

1 large carrot, peeled and diced

1 pound of kielbasa, cut into bite-size pieces

4 minced garlic cloves

4 tablespoons of Ghee

8 chopped slices of bacon

Chopped fresh parsley, for serving

**Preparation:**

- Choose Sauté or Browning on the pressure cooker then adjust to medium heat. Sauté the chopped bacon until it is brown then place them on paper towels so that they will drain. Get the fat out of the pressure cooker.
- Melt the ghee inside the pressure cooker. Add onion, carrot, and garlic then Sauté until the carrot gets soft. After which you can add the apple, sage, salt, thyme, wine, and pepper and cook for a minute or 2 till the liquid reduces by almost half.
- Put the cooked bacon, sauerkraut, broth, and kielbasa in the pressure cooker then mix the ingredients properly, ensuring nothing is left stuck to the pan's bottom.
- Lock the lid properly and put the steam release knob on seal. Adjust pressure to High and time to 5 minutes. Quick release the pressure after cooking then unlock the lid and remove it.
- Top with chopped parsley. Serve the kielbasa and sauerkraut.

**Per Serving Contains:** 377 Calories, 13g Total Carbs, 8g Net Carbs, 23g Total Fat, 17g Protein, 6g Sugar, 5g Fiber.

**Macros:** 21% Protein, 63% Fat, and 16% Carbs

## PORK BELLY

Made easier and faster to prepare using a pressure cooker, pork belly is a complete delicacy on its own.

**Serves:** 8

**Time for Preparation:** 8 minutes

**Sauté:** 10 minutes

**Time for Pressure Cooking:** 30 minutes on High pressure

**Release:** Quick

**Total Time:** 58 minutes

**Gluten-free, Dairy-free, and Nut-free**

**Ingredients:**

¾ cup of dry white wine

½ teaspoon of freshly ground black pepper

1 tablespoon of sea salt

1 tablespoon of paprika

1 tablespoon of dried thyme

1 teaspoon of ground cloves

1 pound of skinless pork belly

1 tablespoon of dried oregano

2 tablespoons of avocado oil

6 minced garlic cloves

**Preparation:**

- Mix the paprika, oregano, cloves, garlic, thyme, salt, and pepper together in a small bowl.
- Use a sharp knife to cut diagonal lines across one way of the pork's fattier side, and do same with the opposite direction so that the fat will have a diamond pattern. Rub the spice mixture on the pork fat.
- Pour the wine into the pressure cooker before putting the pork belly with its spice-rubbed-side facing up. Lock the lid securely and put the steam release knob on seal. Set pressure to High and time to 30 minutes. Then quick release the pressure after cooking.
- Unlock the lid and remove it. Take the pork belly out of the pot and place it on a cutting board. Allow it sit and cool a bit for 5 to 8 minutes. Cut into your desired thickness, which could be ¼-inch thick slices or thereabout.
- Heat the avocado oil inside a large skillet and place on medium-high heat. Add the slices of pork and sear each side for 1 or 2 minutes until it reaches the crispness you prefer.

**Per Serving Contains:** 355 Calories, 2g Total Carbs, 1g Net Carbs, 34g Total Fat, 6g Protein, 0.5g Sugar, 1g Fiber.

**Macros:** 7% Protein, 90% Fat, and 3% Carbs

# PERFECT ITALIAN MEATBALLS

**Serves:** 7

**Time for Preparation:** 15 minutes

**Time for Pressure Cooking:** 10 minutes on High pressure

**Release:** Quick

**Sauté:** 10 minutes

**Total Time:** 50 minutes

**Gluten-free**

**Ingredients:**

½ cup of almond flour

½ cup of minced onion

½ cup of chopped fresh basil

½ teaspoon of red pepper flakes

½ teaspoon of freshly ground black pepper

1 teaspoon of sea salt

1 teaspoon of dried oregano

1 teaspoon of onion powder

1 tablespoon of nutritional yeast

1 cup of freshly grated Parmesan cheese

1 (24-ounce) can of tomato sauce (no sugar added)

1½ pounds of grass-fed ground beef

2 large eggs

2 tablespoons of Ghee

2 tablespoons of red wine

3 cups of chopped fresh spinach

3 tablespoons of extra-virgin olive oil

4 crushed garlic cloves, divided

**Preparation:**

- Beat the eggs in a large bowl. Add the almond flour, onion, oregano, salt, red pepper flakes, beef, nutritional yeast, half of the crushed garlic, onion powder, and black pepper. Combine these ingredients properly then form them into 15 meatballs of about 1½ - 2-inch size.
- Choose Sauté or Browning on the pressure cooker to set heat to medium. Melt the ghee till it shimmers. Add the crushed garlic left and Sauté till it becomes fragrant. Add the tomato sauce as well as a cup of water.
- Allow the sauce to simmer before adding the basil and meatballs.
- Lock the lid properly and set the knob to seal. Adjust the pressure to a High level and time to 10 minutes. Quick release the pressure after cooking. Unlock the lid and remove it.
- Choose Sauté or Browning on the pressure cooker again, then mix the spinach and the red wine in. Sauté it until the spinach starts wilting.
- Top with the grated Parmesan cheese and drizzle this with olive oil. Serve.

**Per Serving Contains:** 477 Calories, 10g Total Carbs, 8g Net Carbs, 36g Total Fat, 28g Protein, 5g Sugar, 2g Fiber.

**Macros:** 24% Protein, 68% Fat, and 8% Carbs

## BARBECUE PULLED PORK

**Serves: 8**

**Time for Preparation: 5 minutes**

**Sauté: 25 minutes**

**Time for Pressure Cooking: 60 minutes on High pressure**

**Release: Natural**

**Total Time: 1 hour 45 minutes**

**Gluten-free and Nut-free**

**Ingredients:**

1 teaspoon of ground cumin

1 teaspoon ground cinnamon

1 tablespoon of garlic powder

1 teaspoon of smoked paprika

1 tablespoon of mustard powder

1 teaspoon of freshly ground black pepper

1 cup of Sugar-Free Barbecue Sauce, and more for serving

2 tablespoons of Ghee

2 teaspoons of sea salt

2 teaspoons of chili powder

4 pounds of pork shoulder, cut into 4 (1-pound) pieces

**Preparation:**

- Get a small bowl and properly mix the garlic powder, chili powder, pepper, cumin, cinnamon, mustard powder, salt, and paprika in it. Place the pork inside a medium bowl then evenly rub the spice all over the pieces.
- Choose Sauté or Browning on the pressure cooker. Set on medium heat and heat up the ghee until shimmering. Work in 2 batches; then put the pieces of pork in a single layer inside the pressure cooker. Cook each batch for 5 minutes by cooking the pork while stirring frequently. When the pork is lightly browned, move to a plate.
- Return the pork into the pressure cook, then add ½ cup of water and a cup of barbecue sauce. Stir and mix very well.
- Lock the lid and place the steam release knob on seal. Adjust to High pressure and adjust time to 60 minutes. Naturally release the pressure after cooking. Unlock the lid and remove it.
- With utmost care, take out the pork and place it in a large bowl. Use two forks to shred the meat. Return it to the pressure cooker to cook on high pressure for extra 10 to 20 minutes if it does not early shred, before putting it back in the bowl and shredding.
- Choose Sauté or Browning on the pressure cooker then cook the sauce remaining in the cooker for 10 to 15 minutes. When it has reduced by about

half, put the shredded pork in the sauce and mix properly. Serve it with barbecue sauce.

**Per Serving Contains:** 414 Calories, 7g Total Carbs, 6g Net Carbs, 28g Total Fat, 37g Protein, 5g Sugar, 1g Fiber.

**Macros:** 34% Protein, 59% Fat, and 7% Carbs

## PORK GYRO LETTUCE WRAPS WITH TZATZIKI

Best paired with fresh feta cheese and sliced olives, these lettuce wraps comprise of tender pork, onions that are really soft, as well as fresh cucumber tzatziki sauce.

**Serves:** 8

**Time for Preparation:** 5 minutes

**Sauté:** 2 minutes

**Time for Pressure Cooking:** 25 minutes on High pressure

**Release:** 10 minutes Natural, then Quick

**Total Time:** 52 minutes

**Gluten-free and Nut-free**

**Ingredients for the Pork Lettuce Wraps**

¼ cup of bone broth or beef broth

¼ teaspoon of freshly ground black pepper

½ cup of crumbled feta cheese

½ cup of sliced Kalamata olives

½ cup of freshly squeezed lemon juice

1 sliced onion

1 teaspoon of sea salt

1 teaspoon of dried marjoram

1 teaspoon of dried rosemary

2 tablespoons of minced garlic

3 pounds of boneless pork shoulder, cut into 1-inch cubes

4 tablespoons of Ghee, at room temperature, divided

16 romaine lettuce leaves

**Ingredients for the Tzatziki**

¼ teaspoon of freshly ground black pepper

½ teaspoon of sea salt

½ cup of full-fat Greek yogurt

1 minced garlic clove

1 teaspoon of paprika

1 small diced cucumber

1 teaspoon of dried oregano

1 teaspoon of ground cumin

1 cup of full-fat grass-fed sour cream

1½ tablespoons of freshly squeezed lemon juice

2 tablespoons of fresh dill

**Preparation:**

- Get a medium bowl and put 2 tablespoons of ghee inside, before adding the marjoram, salt, garlic, rosemary, and pepper. Mix properly before adding the pork. Rub the ghee mixture all over the pork and set aside.
- Choose Sauté or browning on the pressure cooker then set on medium heat. Melt the 2 tablespoons of ghee remaining until it shimmers. Put in the sliced onion and allow to Sauté for a minute or 2. Include the seasoned pork then pour the bone broth and lemon juice over it. Stir.
- Lock the lid securely and set the steam release knob to seal. Put on high pressure and set time to 25 minutes.

- Make the tzatziki while the pork is cooking by mixing all its ingredients in a small bowl. Set it aside.
- When the pork is done cooking, naturally release the pressure for 10 minutes, then quick release whatever pressure is left. Unlock the lid and remove it. Use a slotted spoon to remove the meat and onions.
- Serve like lettuce wraps and top it with tzatziki, feta cheese and olives.

**Macro Tip:** You can substitute the full-fat Greek yogurt for the sour cream in order to get higher protein and lower fat.

**Per Serving (2 Lettuce Wraps) Contains:** 432 Calories, 11g Total Carbs, 10g Net Carbs, 27g Total Fat, 36g Protein, 3g Sugar, 1g Fiber.

**Macros:** 34% Protein, 56% Fat, and 10% Carbs

## BARBACOA BEEF

**Serves: 8**

**Time for Preparation: 5 minutes**

**Sauté: 13 minutes**

**Time for Pressure Cooking: 60 minutes on High pressure**

**Release: Quick**

**Total Time: 1 hour 20 minutes**

**Dairy-free, Gluten-free, and Nut-free**

**Ingredients:**

¼ cup of chopped fresh cilantro

¼ teaspoon of freshly ground black pepper

½ teaspoon of ground cloves

½ cup of bone broth or beef broth

½ cup of freshly squeezed lime juice

1 minced onion

1 teaspoon of sea salt

1 tablespoon of dried oregano

2 tablespoons of ground cumin

2 tablespoons of apple cider vinegar

2 to 4 minced chipotle chiles in adobo sauce

3 pounds of grass-fed beef brisket, cut into 2- to 3-inch chunks

3 tablespoons of avocado oil

6 minced garlic cloves

**Preparation:**

- Whisk the onion, chipotles, apple cider vinegar, oregano, broth, garlic, lime juice, cumin, and cloves in a small bowl, then set aside.
- Season the chunks of beef with pepper and salt inside a medium bowl. Choose Sauté or browning feature on the pressure cooker. Set on medium heat and heat the avocado oil in it until it shimmers. Include the beef and turn from time to time until most sides are browned; this should take about 6 to 8 minutes. Pour the sauce into the pressure cooker and use a wooden spoon to scrape up browned bits.
- Lock the lid properly and set the steam release knob on seal. Adjust to high pressure and set time on 60 minutes. Quick release the pressure after cooking. Unlock the lid and remove it.
- Use a slotted spoon to transfer the beef to a bowl, then use two forks to shred it. Return it to the sauce. Top with the cilantro and serve.

**Per Serving Contains:** 414 Calories, 5g Total Carbs, 4g Net Carbs, 31g Total Fat, 27g Protein, 1g Sugar, 1g Fiber.

**Macros:** 26% Protein, 69% Fat, and 5% Carbs

## BEEF BOURGUIGNON

**Serves:** 4

**Time for Preparation:** 8 minutes

**Sauté:** 18 minutes

**Time for Pressure Cooking:** 30 minutes on high pressure

**Release:** Quick

**Simmer:** 8 minutes

**Total Time:** 1 hour 6 minutes

**Gluten-free and Nut-free**

**Ingredients:**

¼ cup of chopped fresh parsley

¼ teaspoon of freshly ground black pepper

½ cup of beef bone broth or beef broth

1 bay leaf

1 teaspoon of dried thyme

1 cup of sliced mushrooms

1 to 2 tablespoons of grass-fed beef gelatin or ¼ to ½ teaspoon of xanthan gum (optional)

1½ pounds of grass-fed chuck roast, cut into 1-inch pieces

2 cups of red wine

2 sliced carrots

2 teaspoons of sea salt

2 cups of frozen pearl onions

2 tablespoons of tomato paste

3 tablespoons of unsalted grass-fed butter

6 minced garlic cloves

10 thick bacon slices, chopped

**Preparation:**

- Choose Sauté or browning on the pressure cooker then set to medium heat before you Sauté the bacon until it gets crisp. Drain the bacon on paper towels, and leave the rendered bacon fat inside the cooker.

- Add the beef in small batches and cook to brown on all sides for 3 to 5 minutes. When all sides of the beef are browned, set aside.
- Allow the butter to melt in the pressure cooker until it foams. Add the carrots, mushrooms, and garlic then Sauté for 2 to 3 minutes. Stir occasionally.
- Add the beef, tomato paste, broth, bay leaf, pepper, onions, wine, thyme, and salt to the pressure cooker.
- Lock the lid and set the steam release knob to seal Set the pressure on High and time to 30 minutes. Quick release the pressure after cooking. Unlock the lid and remove it.
- Reset the pressure cooker on Sauté or browning setting. Let the sauce simmer for 6 to 8 minutes. Allow it to thicken and let the alcohol cook off.
- If you like, mix a tablespoon of gelatin into 4 to 5 tablespoons of cold water and allow to sit for a minute. Put half of the gelatin mixture in the sauce and mix until everything dissolves. Keep adding the gelatin until it reaches a consistency you prefer (the gelatin thickens as it cools). Repeat the process with more gelatin and water if desired. If using xanthan gum, put ¼ teaspoon at a time until it thickens. Stir for 1 or 2 more minutes until the sauce becomes thick.
- Stir the bacon into the beef bourguignon. Garnish with the parsley and serve.

**Per Serving Contains:** 583 Calories, 8g Total Carbs, 6g Net Carbs, 28g Total Fat, 33g Protein, 4g Sugar, 2g Fiber.

**Macros:** 31% Protein, 61% Fat, and 8% Carbs

## TACO MEAT

**Serves:** 4

**Time for Preparation:** 2 minutes

**Time for Pressure Cooking:** 18 minutes on High pressure

**Release:** Quick

**Sauté:** 5 minutes

**Total Time:** 35 minutes

**Gluten-free and Nut-free**

**Ingredients:**

¼ teaspoon of cayenne pepper

½ minced onion

½ teaspoon of sea salt

½ teaspoon of dried oregano

½ teaspoon of ground coriander

½ teaspoon of ground cinnamon

½ teaspoon of freshly ground black pepper

1 tablespoon of onion powder

1 tablespoon of ground cumin

1¼ pounds of frozen grass-fed ground beef

2 cups of Guacamole

2 tablespoons of Ghee

2 teaspoons of chili powder

2 teaspoons of smoked paprika

3 minced garlic cloves

4 cups of mixed salad greens

4 tablespoons of dairy-free sour cream

**Preparation:**

- Pour a cup of water into the pressure cooker. Place the trivet inside the cooker and place the frozen beef on it.
- Lock the lid and seal the steam release knob. Set on high pressure and set time to 18 minutes. Quick release the pressure after cooking. Unlock the lid and remove it.
- Use tongs to remove the beef and set it aside. The beef does not have to be completely cooked at this point, as it will keep cooking in the subsequent steps. Pour off from the pressure cooker accumulated liquids and reserve them.

- Choose Sauté or browning on the pressure cooker then set on medium heat and allow the ghee heat until it shimmers. Add the onion and garlic and Sauté until they are fragrant.
- Put the beef back into the pressure cooker and use a wooden spoon to crumble. Sauté until it is well cooked. Add ¼ cup of the cooking liquid you reserved, then add the cumin, onion powder, paprika, cinnamon, sea salt, chili powder, cayenne pepper, coriander, oregano, and black pepper. Sauté until most of the liquid evaporates.
- Place the taco meat on mixed greens, then use the guacamole and sour cream as toppings. Serve.

**Per Serving Contains:** 582 Calories, 23g Total Carbs, 10g Net Carbs, 52g Total Fat, 39g Protein, 3g Sugar, 13g Fiber.

**Macros:** 23% Protein, 65% Fat, and 12% Carbs

## FALL-OFF-THE-BONE BABY BACK RIBS

**Serves:** 4

**Time for Preparation:** 8 minutes

**Time for Pressure Cooking:** 25 minutes on high pressure

**Broil Time:** 5 minutes

**Release:** Natural

**Total Time:** 1 hour

Dairy-free, Gluten-free, and Nut-free

**Ingredients:**

¼ teaspoon of liquid smoke

¼ cup of apple cider vinegar

½ teaspoon of cayenne pepper

1 tablespoon of paprika

1 rack of baby back pork ribs

1 tablespoon of onion powder

1 tablespoon of garlic powder

1 cup of sugar-free barbecue sauce, divided

2 tablespoons of chili powder

2 teaspoons of dried oregano

**Preparation:**

- Get a small bowl and mix the garlic powder, chili powder oregano, paprika, onion powder, and cayenne powder in it. Set aside.
- Insert the tip of a knife under the skin to remove the membrane from the rib's bottom side. Grip the membrane and remove it completely. Evenly rub the spice mixture over the ribs.
- Pour a cup of water into the pressure cooker then add liquid smoke and cider vinegar. Place the trivet in the cooker and keep the ribs on top.
- Lock the lid properly and set the steam release knob to seal. Set pressure on High level and time to 25 minutes. Naturally release the pressure after cooking. Unlock the lid and remove it.
- Let the oven preheat to broil. Then use parchment paper to line the baking sheet.
- Carefully take out the ribs from the pressure cooker and place it on the baking sheet already prepared. Use ½ cup of barbecue sauce to brush then broil for 3 to 5 minutes. Get them out of the oven then serve hot with the remaining barbecue sauce for dipping.

**Per Serving Contains:** 511 Calories, 12g Total Carbs, 8g Net Carbs, 31g Total Fat, 22g Protein, 4g Sugar, 4g Fiber.

**Macros:** 22% Protein, 66% Fat, and 12% Carbs

# HAWAIIAN PORK

**Serves: 8**

**Time for Preparation: 3 minutes**

**Sauté: 5 minutes**

**Time for Pressure Cooking: 90 minutes on High pressure**

**Release: Natural**

**Total Time:** 1 hour 48 minutes

**Dairy-free, Gluten-free, and Nut-free**

**Ingredients:**

1 tablespoon of coconut aminos

2 teaspoons of liquid smoke

2 tablespoons of coconut oil

2 teaspoons of pink Himalayan sea salt

4 pounds of pork shoulder, cut into 2 pieces

6 peeled garlic cloves

**Preparation:**

- Choose the Sauté or browning feature on the pressure cooker, then set heat to medium. Heat the coconut oil until it shimmers, then add the pork to brown on all sides for about 5 minutes. Take the pork out of the pressure cooker and place it on a work surface to cool a bit.
- Use a sharp knife to cut 3 slips into each of the pork pieces then press the garlic cloves in. Evenly sprinkle the pink Himalayan sea salt over the pork.
- Pour ½ cup of water into the pressure cooker then add the liquid smoke, coconut aminos, and the browned pork.
- Lock the lid securely then set the steam release knob to seal. Set pressure on high and time on 90 minutes. Naturally release the pressure after cooking. Unlock the lid and remove it.
- Use tongs to take the pork out of the pressure cooker and into a large bowl. Use 2 forks to shred the pork. Serve.

**Per Serving (½ Pound) Contains:** 517 Calories, 1g Total Carbs, 1g Net Carbs, 36g Total Fat, 44g Protein, 1g Sugar, 0g Fiber.

**Macros:** 35% Protein, 64% Fat, and 1% Carbs

# CRISPY PORK CARNITAS

Comprised of both citrus and garlic flavors, this dish is very tender and juicy. It takes about an hour to prepare and is best served on a bed of greens and a serving of guacamole.

**Serves:** 8

**Time for Preparation:** 15 minutes

**Time for Pressure Cooking:** 30 minutes on High pressure

**Release:** Natural

**Total Time:** 1 hour, 10 minutes

**Gluten-free and Nut-free**

**Ingredients:**

¾ cup of chicken broth

¼ cup of chopped fresh cilantro

¼ cup of freshly squeezed lime juice

½ cup of freshly squeezed orange juice

½ teaspoon of freshly ground black pepper

1 bay leaf

1 teaspoon of sea salt

1 teaspoon of chili powder

1 cup of thinly sliced onion

1 teaspoon of dried oregano

1 tablespoon of ground cumin

3½ pounds of boneless pork roast, excess fat trimmed, cut into chunks

4 cups of Guacamole

4 cups of mixed greens

4 tablespoons of divided Ghee

6 minced garlic cloves

**Preparation:**

- Combine the cumin, chili powder, pepper, oregano, and sea salt. Place the chunks of pork in a large bowl, then use the seasoning mixture to sprinkle before tossing to coat the pork.
- Pour the lime juice, chicken broth, and orange juice into the pressure cooker. Put in the onion, bay leaf, and garlic then stir properly to mix. Add the pork that has been spice-coated to the pot.
- Lock the lid and set the steam release knob on seal. Set on High pressure and adjust time to 30 minutes. Naturally release the pressure after cooking. Unlock the lid and remove it. Use a slotted spoon to move the pork to a medium bowl. Do not get rid of the liquid in the pressure cooker. Use 2 forks to shred the pork meat.
- Place 2 tablespoons of ghee in a large skillet and heat over high heat. Add the pork that has been shredded to the pan in small batches then sear until the pork begins to get crispy. Pour ½ cup of leftover liquid from the pressure cooker on the pork then keep searing until the liquid evaporates. Move to a platter. Repeat until you have seared all the pork then use the remaining ghee as needed.
- Pour more of the cooking liquid left on the seared pork and top with chopped cilantro.
- Place the carnitas on mixed greens and use guacamole to top. Serve.

**Cooking Tip:** To make this dish a one-pot one, use Sauté or browning on the pressure cooker. After shredding the pork, move the cooking liquid to another bowl and pur the pressure cooker on Sauté or browning. Heat a tablespoon or 2 of ghee in the cooker until it shimmers, and put the shredded pork. Use a cup of leftover liquid to Sauté until the meat becomes crisp and the liquid evaporates.

**Per Serving Contains:** 559 Calories, 17g Total Carbs, 8g Net Carbs, 34g Total Fat, 46g Protein, 2g Sugar, 9g Fiber.

**Macros:** 33% Protein, 55% Fat, and 12% Carbs

## PHILLY CHEESESTEAK

Made from thinly sliced steak pieces, melted cheese, onions and pepper, this variation of the classic Philadelphia cheesesteak is absolutely keto-friendly.

**Serves:** 6

**Time for Preparation:** 5 minutes

**Sauté:** 13 minutes

**Time for Pressure Cooking:** 4 minutes on high pressure

**Release:** Quick

**Broil:** 3 minutes

**Total Time:** 35 minutes

**Gluten-free and Nut-free**

**Ingredients:**

2 tablespoons of unsalted grass-fed butter

2 large sliced yellow onions

1 teaspoon of sea salt, divided

4 minced garlic cloves

3 green bell peppers, sliced

2 pounds of thinly sliced grass-fed sirloin steak

½ teaspoon of freshly ground black pepper

1 tablespoon of onion powder

1 tablespoon of Worcestershire sauce

1 teaspoon of dried oregano

½ cup of bone broth or beef broth

6 provolone cheese slices

**Preparation:**

- Choose Sauté or browning on the pressure cooker then set heat to medium, and heat the butter until it foams. Add the onions and ½ teaspoon of salt then Sauté for 8 to 10 minutes. When it is browned, add garlic and bell peppers

then Sauté for 2 to 3 minutes. As soon as the peppers get soft, take out the vegetables from the pressure cooker and set it aside.
- Add the sliced steak and use the remaining ½ teaspoon of salt, onion powder, pepper, oregano, and Worcestershire sauce. Pour the broth in.
- Lock the lid securely then set the steam release knob to seal. Set pressure on High and time to 4 minutes. Quick release the pressure after cooking. Unlock the lid and remove it.
- Put the onions and pepper into the steak and stir until it is heated through.
- Get the oven preheated to broil. Use parchment paper to line the baking sheet.
- Use a slotted spoon to place the meat and vegetables on the prepared baking sheet. Top with cheese slices and allow to broil for 2 to 3 minutes. Serve after the cheese melts.

**Preparation Tip:** To make the beef easier to slice into very thin strips, allow it freeze for 30 minutes.

**Per Serving Contains:** 566 Calories, 12g Total Carbs, 8g Net Carbs, 39g Total Fat, 40g Protein, 5g Sugar, 4g Fiber.

**Macros:** 29% Protein, 62% Fat, and 9% Carbs

# DESSERTS

# MINI COCONUT-RICOTTA CUSTARD CUPS

This dish is great for lovers of coconut. It beautifully combines a hint of nutrient-rich coconut milk with toasted coconut to create an amazing flavor.

**Serves:** 6

**Time for Preparation:** 10 minutes

**Time for Pressure Cooking:** 6 minutes on High pressure

**Release:** Natural for 10 minutes, then Quick

**Total Time:** 35 minutes, with additional 2 to 4 hours for chilling

**Gluten-free, Nut-free, and Vegetarian**

**Ingredients:**

⅔ cup of full-fat ricotta cheese

⅔ cup of Swerve granulated sweetener

½ cup of coconut milk

½ cup of toasted unsweetened shredded coconut

1 teaspoon of vanilla extract

2 large eggs with 2 large egg yolks

8 ounces of softened cream cheese

**Preparation:**

- Put the cream cheese, coconut milk, and ricotta in a medium bowl, then use a handheld electric mixer to beat them until it gets smooth. Include the Swerve and vanilla then beat some more until it gets very smooth. Include the whole eggs and egg yolks and beat some more to blend. Stir the shredded coconut in.
- Evenly pour the custard mixture into six 1- to 1½-cup of ramekins, with a space of about ½ inch left at the top of each ramekin. Use aluminum foil to cover the ramekins.
- Pour a cup of water into the pressure cooker then place the trivet in it. Keep 3 of the ramekins on the trivet. Heap the 3 remaining ramekins on them, slightly staggering them.

- Lock the lid securely and set the steam release knob to seal. Adjust pressure level to High and time to 6 minutes. Naturally release the pressure for 10 minutes after cooking, then quick release any pressure left. Unlock the lid and remove it.
- Get the foil off one of the ramekins very carefully to check if the custard is done. If the center isn't well set, relock the pressure cooker lid and cook on high pressure for additional 5 minutes. Get the ramekins off very carefully and get rid of the foil. Allow the custards to cool. Cover it with a plastic wrap and refrigerate for 2 to 4 hours. Serve chill.

**Per Serving Contains:** 276 Calories, 5g Total Carbs, 5g Net Carbs, 2g Total Fat, 9g Protein, 3g Sugar, 1g Fiber.

**Macros:** 13% Protein, 80% Fat, and 7% Carbs

# LEMON CUSTARD

This summer dessert is prepared with recipes that bring out light citrus flavors to refresh you.

**Serves: 4**

**Time for Preparation: 5 minutes**

**Time for Pressure Cooking: 10 minutes on High pressure**

**Release: Quick**

**Total Time: 25 minutes, with 2 hours for chilling**

**Gluten-free, Nut-free, and Vegetarian**

**Ingredients:**

½ teaspoon of liquid stevia or ½ cup of preferred powdered sugar substitute

1 cup of mixed fresh berries

1 cup of full-fat coconut cream

1 teaspoon of vanilla extract

2 teaspoons of finely grated lemon zest

3 tablespoons of freshly squeezed lemon juice

3 tablespoons of unsalted grass-fed butter, at room temperature

4 large egg yolks with 1 large egg

**Preparation:**

- Mix the coconut cream, whole egg, egg yolks, stevia, butter, vanilla, lemon zest, and lemon juice until it is smooth.
- Pour the mixture into a 7-inch round pan that will fit well into the pressure cooker. Cover with a foil very tightly.
- Pour a cup of water into the pressure cooker and put the trivet in it. Use aluminum foil to make a sling by folding a long lengthwise piece of foil into thirds. Lower the custard pan onto the trivet with a sling.
- Lock the lid properly and position the steam release knob to seal. Set on high pressure and set time to 10 minutes. Quick release the pressure after cooking. Unlock the lid and remove it.
- Use the foil sling to carefully get the custard pan out of the pressure cooker. Remove the foil and get rid of it. Put the custard in the refrigerator to chill for an hour or 2. Serve with fresh berries.

**Per Serving Contains:** 267 Calories, 9g Total Carbs, 7g Net Carbs, 24g Total Fat, 6g Protein, 5g Sugar, 2g Fiber.

**Macros:** 9% Protein, 78% Fat, and 13% Carbs

## CRÈME BRULEE

**Serves: 6**

**Time for Preparation: 5 minutes**

**Time for Pressure Cooking: 6 minutes on high pressure**

**Release: Natural for 10 minutes, then Quick**

**Broil: 10 minutes**

**Total Time: 40 minutes, with 2 to 4 hours to chill**

**Gluten-free, Nut-free, and Vegetarian**

**Ingredients:**

⅛ teaspoon of sea salt

½ cup of fresh raspberries

½ teaspoon of liquid stevia or preferred powdered sugar substitute equivalent to ½ cup sugar

1 teaspoon of vanilla extract

2 cups of heavy cream

6 large egg yolks

6 tablespoons of powdered sugar substitute, for topping (use one with a 1:1 substitution ratio to sugar)

Unsalted grass-fed butter, for greasing

**Preparation:**

- Grease 6 ramekins lightly with butter.
- Whisk the egg yolks, salt, and stevia together in a medium bowl. Add the vanilla extract and cream and mix until it is very smooth. Pour the mixture into the already prepared ramekins. Use the aluminum foil to cover each ramekin.
- Pour a cup of water into the pressure cooker and put the trivet in it. Keep 3 of the ramekins on the trivet. Heap the 3 ramekins left on them.
- Lock the lid securely and set the steam release knob to seal. Set to high pressure and time to 6 minutes. Naturally release the pressure for 10 minutes after cooking, then quick release the pressure left. Unlock the lid and remove it.
- Carefully take the ramekins out of the pressure cooker and get rid of the foil. Leave to cool. Use plastic wrap to cover and then refrigerate for 2 or 4 hours.
- Take the ramekins out of the refrigerator and top each of them with a tablespoon of powdered sugar substitute. Use a kitchen torch to move the flame 2 inches above each of the custard's surfaces until they form a crust that is hard and caramelized. Allow to cool then top with raspberries and serve.

**Ingredient Substitution:** To make this dessert dairy-free, use coconut oil to grease the ramekins instead of butter. Also, you can use coconut cream instead of heavy cream.

**Per Serving Contains:** 336 Calories, 4g Total Carbs, 3g Net Carbs, 34g Total Fat, 4g Protein, 3g Sugar, 1g Fiber.

**Macros:** 6% Protein, 91% Fat, and 3% Carbs

# KEY LIME PIE

**Serves: 6**

**Time for Preparation: 20 minutes**

**Time for Pressure Cooking: 15 minutes on high pressure**

**Release: Natural for 10 minutes, then Quick**

**Total Time: 55 minutes, with at least 4 hours for chilling**

**Gluten-free and Vegetarian**

**Ingredients for the Crust**

1 cup of almond flour

4 tablespoons of unsalted grass-fed butter, melted, plus more for greasing

6 to 8 teaspoons of liquid stevia or preferred powdered sugar substitute equivalent to 1

tablespoon sugar

Ingredients for the Filling

½ cup of full-fat sour cream

½ cup of freshly squeezed Key lime juice

1⅓ cups of Sugar-Free Sweetened Condensed Milk

3 tablespoons of finely grated Key lime zest

4 large egg yolks

**Ingredients for the Topping**

1 cup of heavy cream

1 teaspoon of vanilla extract

1 tablespoon of finely grated Key lime zest, for garnish (optional)

6 to 8 teaspoons of liquid stevia or preferred powdered sugar substitute equivalent to 1

tablespoon sugar

**To Make the Crust**

Grease a 7-inch springform pan and butter.

Get a small bowl and mix the almond flour, stevia, and 4 tablespoons of butter.

Evenly mix the mixture into the bottom and the side of the springform pan. Let the piecrust freeze for 15 minutes.

**To Make the Filling**

- Get a medium bowl and use a handheld electric mixer to beat the egg yolks in it for 2 to 3 minutes. When the pale yellow begins to thicken, keep mixing and gradually add the lime juice, condensed milk, lime zest, and sour cream. Keep mixing until it gets smooth. Pour the pie filling in the crust that is in the springform pan then cover it with aluminum foil.
- Pour a cup of water into the pressure cooker then place the trivet into it.
- Use an aluminum foil to make a sling by folding the long piece into thirds. Lower the springform pan into the cooker with the help of the sling.
- Lock the lid properly and set the steam release knob on seal. Set pressure level to high and time to 15 minutes. Naturally release the pressure for 10 minutes after cooking, then quick release the pressure left. Unlock the lid and remove it.
- Use the foil sling to get the pie out of the pressure cooker very carefully. Allow it cool at room temperature for 10 to 15 minutes, before putting it in the refrigerator for at least 4 hours or overnight so it can chill until you are ready to serve.

**To Make the Topping**

When it is about 20 minutes before time for serving, put a metal mixing bowl inside the freezer for about 15 minutes. Get the bowl out and add the stevia, vanilla, and cream, then use the handheld electric mixer to beat for about 1 to 2 minutes until the medium peaks form. Serve the pie immediately with the whipped cream, then use lime zest (optional) to garnish.

**Per Serving Contains:** 270 Calories, 8g Total Carbs, 7g Net Carbs, 25g Total Fat, 4g Protein, 3g Sugar, 1g Fiber.

**Macros:** 5% Protein, 83% Fat, and 12% Carbs

## MARBLED PUMPKIN CHEESECAKE

**Serves:** 8

**Time for Preparation:** 10 minutes

**Time for Pressure Cooking:** 30 minutes on High pressure

**Release:** Natural for 10 minutes, then Quick

**Total Time:** 1 hour, with 4 to 5 hours to chill

**Gluten-free and Vegetarian**

**Ingredients for the Crust**

1 cup of finely chopped pecans, toasted

1 tablespoon of Swerve granulated sweetener

2 tablespoons unsalted grass-fed butter, softened

**Ingredients for the Filling**

½ cup of Swerve granulated sweetener

1 cup of pumpkin purée

1¼ teaspoon of pumpkin pie spice

2 large eggs

6 tablespoons of full-fat sour cream, at room temperature

8 ounces of cream cheese, softened

**Preparation of the Crust**

- Process the pecans in a food processor and swerve till the nuts are well chopped. Add the butter then process till it forms a coarse paste.
- Put the mixture into a 7-inch spring-foam pan's bottom and up its side to about ½-inch. Allow the crust to chill in the refrigerator while you prepare the filling.

**Preparation of the Filling**

- Get a medium bowl and put the cream cheese and sour cream in it, then use a handheld electric mixer to beat it until it becomes very smooth. Put in the Swerve and beat it until it gets smooth. Add the eggs and beat to blend properly. Take out about 1/3 cup of the cream cheese mixture then set aside. Add the pumpkin pie spice and the pumpkin puree to the mixture inside the bowl then beat till it blends well.
- Pour the pumpkin mixture on the crust inside the spring-form pan. Evenly put 5 or 6 spoonfuls of the cream cheese mixture reserved on the pumpkin mixture. Drag a skewer or knife through the dollops of cream cheese to make a marbleized pattern on top of it.
- Pour a cup of water into the pressure cooker than put the trivet with handles into it. Put the spring-form pan on the trivet. Use the aluminum foil to make a sling by folding the foil lengthwise into thirds. Lower the pan to the trivet using the sling. Lock the lid securely and seal the steam release knob. Set on high pressure and set time to 30 minutes. Naturally release the pressure for 10 minutes after cooking, then quick release any pressure left. Unlock the lid and remove it.
- Remove the cheesecake carefully from the pressure cooker then take the foil off. Check the cheesecake with a skewer to be sure it is done. Test the center with the skewer and return to the pressure cooker if it is not quite done. Close the lid, lock it and allow it to sit for some minutes without pressure.
- Allow the cheesecake to cool at room temperature for 15 to 20 minutes, before refrigerating for 4 to 5 hours to completely set before you serve.

**Per Serving Contains:** 272 Calories, 6g Total Carbs, 4g Net Carbs, 26g Total Fat, 5g Protein, 3g Sugar, 2g Fiber.

**Macros:** 8% Protein, 83% Fat, and 9% Carbs

# CHOCOLATE MOUSSE

**Serves:** 4

**Time for Preparation:** 5 minutes

**Time for Pressure Cook:** 10 minutes on High pressure

**Release:** 5 minutes natural, then Quick

**Total Time:** 25 minutes, with at least 3 hours for chilling

**Gluten-free, Nut-free, and Vegetarian**

**Ingredients:**

¼ teaspoon of pink Himalayan sea salt

¼ teaspoon of liquid stevia or ¼ cup preferred powdered sugar substitute

½ cup of whole milk

½ cup of fresh raspberries

1 cup of whipped cream, for serving

1½ cups of heavy cream

2 teaspoons of vanilla extract

5 large eggs yolks

6 ounces of Lily's stevia-sweetened chocolate chips or chopped sugar-free chocolate

**Preparation:**

- Get a medium saucepan and put the cream and milk in it. Allow to simmer over medium heat. Once it simmers, get the pot off the heat and include the chocolate. Whisk until it is melted and very smooth.
- Whisk the stevia, pink Himalayan sea salt, egg yolks, and vanilla together in a large bowl. Continue stirring while pouring the chocolate mixture into the yolk mixture in a thin stream.
- Pour the yolk mixture and chocolate into 4 or 5 heatproof dessert glasses or ramekins. If the 5 glasses do not fit properly, pressure cook the ones left separately without changing the cooking time. You can make this recipe with individual glass ramekins or a spring-form pan; whichever you choose will determine the cooking time. Ramekins, however, are preferred in most cases.

- Pour 2 cups of water into the cooker then put the trivet in it. Neatly place the glasses on the trivet.
- Lock the lid and adjust the steam release knob to seal. Set pressure on high and set time to 10 minutes. Naturally release the pressure for 5 minutes after cooking, then quick release any pressure left. Unlock the lid and remove it.
- Allow the glasses to cool in the pressure cooker for 5 to 8 minutes before you take them out. Either refrigerate overnight or for a minimum of 3 hours. Serve topped with whipped cream and raspberries.

**Per Serving Contains:** 421 Calories, 17g Total Carbs, 9g Net Carbs, 37g Total Fat, 7g Protein, 3g Sugar, 8g Fiber.

**Macros:** 7% Protein, 77% Fat, and 16% Carbs

## CHEESECAKE

**Serves:** 6

**Time for Preparation:** 15 minutes

**Time for Pressure Cooking:** 35 minutes on high pressure

**Release:** Natural

**Total Time:** 1 hour 10 minutes, with additional 6 to 8 hours for chilling

**Gluten-free and Vegetarian**

**Ingredients for the Crust:**

½ teaspoon of sea salt

⅓ cup of almond flour

⅓ cup of shredded coconut

1 cup of macadamia nuts

3 tablespoons of unsalted grass-fed butter, plus more for greasing

6 to 9 drops of liquid stevia or preferred powdered sugar substitute equivalent to 1 tablespoon of sugar

**Ingredients for the Filling**

¼ teaspoon of liquid stevia or ¼ cup of preferred powdered sugar substitute

½ cup of organic sour cream

1 tablespoon of vanilla extract

1 tablespoon of freshly squeezed lemon juice

2 large eggs, at room temperature

16 ounces of cream cheese, at room temperature

Finely grated zest of 1 lemon

**Ingredients for the Topping**

½ cup of sour cream

1 teaspoon of preferred powdered sugar substitute

**Preparation of the Crust**

- Get the oven preheated to 350oF. Use butter to grease a 7-inch spring-form pan.
- Pulse the macadamia nuts in a food processor till they are crushed. Get a small bowl and mix the almond flour, stevia, 3 tablespoons of butter, shredded coconut, salt, and crushed macadamias in it. Evenly press the mixture into the bottom and sides of the spring-form pan.
- Let the crust bake in the oven for 8 minutes, then get them out and allow them cool.

**Preparation of the Filling**

- Prepare the filling while the crust is baking in the oven. Get a medium bowl and mix the cream cheese, lemon juice, vanilla extract, stevia, sour cream, and lemon zest inside. Blend until it is smooth with the help of a handheld electric mixer. Add the egg, one at a time, and mix gently. Overmixing the cheesecake will make it lose its desired creamy texture. As soon as it combines, pour the cheesecake filling into the crust which is in the spring-form pan, then use aluminum foil to cover.
- Pour a cup of water into the pressure cooker, then put the trivet in it.
- Use aluminum foil to make a sling by folding the long foil piece into thirds. Lower the spring-form pan on the trivet which is in the pressure cooker using a sling.

- Lock the lid properly and set the steam release knob on seal. Adjust to high pressure and set time on 35 minutes.
- Naturally release the pressure after cooking. Unlock the lid and remove it.
- Make use of the foil sling to carefully take the cheesecake out of the pressure cooker. Dab moisture off the top of the cake very carefully using a paper tower.

**Preparation of the Topping**

- Prepare the topping while the cheesecake is cooking. Get a small bowl and mix the sour cream and sugar substitute in it. Set the bowl aside.
- Evenly spread the topping over the cheesecake while it is still hot.
- Put the cheesecake in a refrigerator to chill for 6 to 8 hours before you serve.

**Preparation Tip:** If you are short on time, you can make this a crustless cheesecake. Do this by using parchment paper to line the spring-form pan. Doing this will drop the calories to 381 per serving, and reduce the total carbs to 9 grams for each serving.

**Per Serving Contains:** 594 Calories, 16g Total Carbs, 11g Net Carbs, 25g Total Fat, 1g Protein, 5g Sugar, 5g Fiber.

**Macros:** 8% Protein, 82% Fat, and 10% Carbs

# BASICS

## BONE BROTH

Loaded with amazing health benefits, bone broth is a major staple that improves gut health, boosts the immune system, improve the skin and hair condition, and also cushion joints. It substitutes water and even stock for cooking stews and soups.

**Serves: 10 to 12**

**Time for Preparation: 10 minutes**

**Roast: 30 minutes**

**Time for Pressure Cooking: 2 hours on High pressure**

**Release: Natural**

**Total Time: 3 hours 30 minutes**

**Dairy-free, Gluten-free, and Nut-free**

**Ingredients:**

½ teaspoon of whole black peppercorns

1 onion, peeled and halved

1 tablespoon of apple cider vinegar

2 chopped carrots

2 chopped celery stalks

2 teaspoons of pink Himalayan sea salt

2 or 3 herb sprigs (rosemary, sage, parsley, thyme)

2½ pounds of assorted combination of organic chicken or beef bones

5 peeled garlic cloves

**Preparation:**

- Get the oven preheated to 450oF.
- Arrange the bones on a rimmed baking sheet in a single layer, then roast them for 30 to 35 minutes.
- Move the bones to the pressure cooker. Add the carrots, garlic, apple cider vinegar, peppercorns, onion, celery, herb sprigs, and salt. Cover 2/3 of the pressure cooker with water.
- Lock the lid and seal the steam release knob. Set pressure to High and time to 120 minutes. Naturally release the pressure after cooking. Unlock the lid and remove it.
- Place a strainer or cheesecloth-lined colander on a large pot or bowl, then strain the broth and get rid of the bones and vegetables. You can choose to either enjoy it immediately, or allow the broth cool and store it in mason jars that are tightly closed in the refrigerator for about 5 days.

**Ingredient Tip:** Save and freeze the bones gotten when cooking whole chicken, bone-in beef, or chicken thighs. These bones can be used for bone broth.

**Per Serving Contains:** 57 Calories, 1g Total Carbs, 1g Net Carbs, 2g Total Fat, 5g Protein, 0g Sugar, 0g Fiber.

**Macros:** 22% Protein, 37% Fat, and 41% Carbs

# SIMPLE SHREDDED CHICKEN

These staples come in very handy when you need to make meals that are quick and easy, like salads and stir-fries. It could also be served with avocado range dressing and guacamole as toppings for a 5-minute meal.

**Serves: 6**

**Time for Preparation: 2 minutes**

**Time for Pressure Cooking: 13 minutes on high pressure**

**Release: Quick**

**Total Time: 25 minutes**

**Dairy-free, Nut-free, and Gluten-free**

**Ingredients:**

½ teaspoon of freshly ground black pepper

1 teaspoon of sea salt

1 teaspoon of garlic powder

2 pounds of boneless chicken thighs

**Preparation:**

- Use pepper, garlic powder, and salt to season both sides of the chicken thighs generously.
- Move the chicken thighs to the pressure cooker, then add ½ cup of water.
- Lock the lid and set the steam release knob on seal. Set to high pressure and set time to 13 minutes. Quick release the pressure after cooking. Unlock the lid and remove it.
- Use 2 forks to get the chicken out of the pot and shred. Place in airtight glass storage container and store by refrigerating for 3 to 4 days, or by freezing for 2 to 4 months.

**Per Serving Contains:** 178 Calories, 1g Total Carbs, 1g Net Carbs, 6g Total Fat, 30g Protein, 0g Sugar, 0g Fiber.

**Macros:** 67% Protein, 31% Fat, and 3% Carbs

## ZUCCHINI NOODLES

Also known as Zoodles, Zucchini noodles serve as the best base for a lot of recipes. Zoodles substitute pasta quite perfectly and are best paired with shrimp scampi or the perfect Italian meatballs.

**Serves: 4**

**Time for Preparation: 5 minutes**

**Time for Cooking: 5 minutes**

**Total Time: 10 minutes**

**Gluten-free, Nut-free, and Vegetarian**

**Ingredients:**

½ teaspoon of sea salt

½ teaspoon of freshly ground black pepper

2 tablespoons of Ghee

2 medium Zucchini

**Preparation:**

- Use a knife, julienne peeler, or spiralizer to cut the zucchini into strands that are noodle-like.
- Place the ghee in a skillet and melt it over medium heat. As soon as it gets hot, put in the raw zoodles and cook until they become as soft as you desire. Add pepper and salt for seasoning and use any toppings you prefer.

**Per Serving Contains:** 75 Calories, 2g Total Carbs, 1g Net Carbs, 8g Total Fat, 0g Protein, 2g Sugar, 1g Fiber.

**Macros:** 1% Protein, 91% Fat, and 8% Carbs

## GUACAMOLE

**Makes: 3 cups**

**Total Time: 10 minutes**

**Dairy-free, Gluten-free, Nut-free, and Vegan**

**Ingredients:**

¼ cup of chopped fresh cilantro

¼ teaspoon of ground cayenne pepper

½ minced onion

½ teaspoon of ground cumin

½ jalapeño pepper, seeded and minced

1 minced garlic clove

1 tablespoon of extra-virgin olive oil

6 ripe avocados, halved and pitted

Sea salt

Juice of 3 limes

Freshly ground black pepper

**Preparation:**

- Scoop out the avocado flesh and place in a mixing bowl. Add the onion, garlic, cumin, cayenne, lime juice, cilantro, and jalapeno to the bowl. Season using pepper and salt. Mash with a fork until you get the preferred consistency.
- Drizzle olive oil on the guacamole, then serve.

**Ingredient Tip:** You can add bacon to this for a more keto-based diet. 3 pieces of cooked crumbled bacon added to this guacamole will make it fancier.

**Per Serving (¼ Cup) Contains:** 133 Calories, 8g Total Carbs, 3g Net Carbs, 12g Total Fat, 2g Protein, 1g Sugar, 5g Fiber.

**Macros:** 4% Protein, 74% Fat, and 22% Carbs

## SUGAR-FREE BARBECUE SAUCE

This is a simple recipe that contains low carbs but remains sweet, tangy and smoky.

**Makes:** 1½ cups

**Time for Preparation:** 5 minutes

**Time for Cooking:** 20 minutes

**Total Time:** 25 minutes

**Gluten-free and Nut-free**

**Ingredients:**

¼ cup of apple cider vinegar

¼ to ½ teaspoon of cayenne pepper

⅓ teaspoon of liquid stevia or sugar substitute equivalent to ⅓ cup sugar

½ teaspoon of chili powder

1 teaspoon of sea salt

1 teaspoon of liquid smoke

1 tablespoon of onion powder

1 tablespoon of Dijon mustard

1 tablespoon of garlic powder

1 teaspoon of smoked paprika

1 tablespoon of Worcestershire sauce

2 tablespoons of unsalted grass-fed butter

10 ounces of canned tomato paste

**Preparation:**

- Whisk together ½ cup of water with apple cider vinegar, tomato paste, Worcestershire sauce, butter, garlic powder, salt, onion powder, smoked paprika, chili powder, cayenne, stevia, Dijon mustard, and liquid smoke in a small saucepan. Bring to a boil, then reduce the heat and allow it simmer for 15 minutes while seldom stirring it. Remove from the heat when the sauce reaches the consistency preferred.
- Allow the sauce to cool a bit and taste. You can add more stevia or cayenne to adjust the spice and sweetness to suit your taste. Put in an airtight glass storage jar and place in a refrigerator to chill for about 2 weeks.

**Per Serving Contains:** 52 Calories, 6g Total Carbs, 1g Net Carbs, 3g Total Fat, 2g Protein, 3g Sugar, 5g Fiber.

**Macros:** 1% Protein, 48% Fat, and 41% Carbs

## AVOCADO RANCH DRESSING

This homemade avocado ranch dressing comprises fresh herbs and healthy fats, unlike the store-bought salad dressings that could be quite unhealthy.

**Makes:** 1¼ cups

**Time for Preparation:** 5 minutes

**Total Time:** 8 minutes, with additional 1 to 2 hours for chilling

**Dairy-free, Gluten-free, Nut-free, and Vegetarian**

**Ingredients:**

½ teaspoon of freshly ground black pepper

⅓ cup of avocado oil mayonnaise

⅓ cup of full-fat coconut cream

1 teaspoon of sea salt

1 teaspoon of onion powder

1 tablespoon of chopped fresh dill

1 tablespoon of chopped fresh chives

1 avocado, halved, pitted, peeled, and chopped

2 peeled garlic cloves

2 tablespoons of chopped fresh parsley

2 teaspoons of freshly squeezed lemon juice

**Preparation:**

- Combine all the ingredients in a blender. Blend until it is smooth; this should take about a minute or 2.

- Place in the refrigerator to chill for an hour or 2. You may store the dressing in an airtight jar inside the refrigerator for about a week.

**Per Serving Contains:** 68 Calories, 3g Total Carbs, 1g Net Carbs, 6g Total Fat, 1g Protein, 1g Sugar, 2g Fiber.

**Macros:** 4% Protein, 79% Fat, and 17% Carbs

# GHEE

To make ghee, you have to heat butter so as to separate the fat from the milk solids. Ghee is rich in fatty acids that are useful to the body. It contains no lactose or casein, but has a high smoke point which makes it suitable for cooking at high temperatures.

**Makes: About 1¾ cups**

**Time for Preparation: 1 minute**

**Sauté: 11 minutes**

**Total Time: 12 minutes**

**Gluten-free, Nut-free, and Vegetarian**

**Ingredient:**

1 pound of unsalted grass-fed butter

**Preparation:**

- Choose Sauté or browning on the pressure cooker then set on medium heat. Add the butter then cook for about 7 to 10 minutes, while stirring frequently. When the milk solids separate, turn the pressure cooker off. Allow the ghee to cool for about 5 to 10 minutes.
- Get a glass jar and place a funnel on it. Place a cheesecloth or fine-mesh strainer on the funnel and strain the ghee into the jar. Cover the jar and close it tightly. Store in a refrigerator for about a year, or in a cool place for up to a month.

**Cooking Tip:** The cooking time depends on the quality of the butter and the pressure cooker's temperature. As soon as the butter is clear and the milk solids have settled at the bottom, click Cancel on the pressure cooker. The ghee will continue to cook afterwards, and the milk solids will turn brown.

**Per Serving (1 Tablespoon) Contains:** 120 Calories, 0g Total Carbs, 0g Net Carbs, 14g Total Fat, 0g Protein, 0g Sugar, 0g Fiber.

**Macros:** 0% Protein, 100% Fat, and 0% Carbs

## DAIRY-FREE SOUR CREAM

This is one great recipe that helps reduce dairy intake while increasing fat intake. The sour cream is made from coconut milk and is best paired with mole chicken, three-meat chili, and crispy pork carnitas.

**Makes:** ¾ cup

**Time for Preparation:** 5 minutes

**Total Time:** 5 minutes

**Dairy-free, Gluten-free, Nut-free, and Vegan**

**Ingredients:**

⅛ teaspoon of sea salt, with additional for seasoning

1 teaspoon of onion powder

1 teaspoon of chopped chives

1 tablespoon of freshly squeezed lemon juice

1 (13.5-ounce) can of full-fat coconut milk or ¾ cup of full-fat coconut cream

**Preparation:**

- If you choose to use coconut milk, let the can of milk refrigerate for a minimum of 6 hours so that the cream will separate. Open the can and scrape the cream alone into a medium bowl. However, if you are using coconut cream, measure out ¾ cup of the cream and place it in a bowl.
- Whisk in the onion powder, lemon juice, chives, onion powder, and sea salt until they are properly mixed to your preferred consistency. If needed, add more salt for seasoning.

**Per Serving Contains:** 45 Calories, 1g Total Carbs, 1g Net Carbs, 5g Total Fat, 1g Protein, 1g Sugar, 0g Fiber.

**Macros:** 5% Protein, 90% Fat, and 5% Carbs

# 3 MONTHS WEIGHT LOSS PLAN

## WEEK 1

|        | SUN | MON | TUE | WED | THUR | FRI | SAT |
|--------|-----|-----|-----|-----|------|-----|-----|
| B/FAST | Scotch Eggs | Shakshuka | Egg Cups | Egg Muffins | Tomato Frittata | Avocado Eggs Benedict | Almond Bread |
| LUNCH  | Chicken Shawarma | Chicken Pho | Honey Turkey Breast | Easy Lobster Bisque | Pork Belly | Mole Chicken | Taco Meat |
| DINNER | Cheese Cake | Lemon Custard | Chocolate Mousse | Beef Stew | Tom Kha Gai | Chunky Clam Chowder | Collard Greens |

## WEEK 2

|        | SUN | MON | TUE | WED | THUR | FRI | SAT |
|--------|-----|-----|-----|-----|------|-----|-----|
| B/FAST | Omelet with Chives | Palak Paneer | Egg Loaf | Baba Ghanoush | Tomato Frittata | Poblano and Cheese Frittata | Coconut Yogurt |
| LUNCH  | Lobster Tail | Garlic Chicken Pieces | Keto Chicken Thigh | Taco Meat | Barbacoa Beef | Hawaiian Pork | Philly Cheese Steak |
| DINNER | Tom Kha Gai | White Chicken Chili | No-Noodle Chicken Soup | Crème Brulee | Chocolate Mousse | Key Lime Pie | Marbled Pumpkin Cheesecake |

## WEEK 3

|        | SUN | MON | TUE | WED | THUR | FRI | SAT |
|--------|-----|-----|-----|-----|------|-----|-----|
| B/FAST | Shakashuka | Baba Ghanoush | Scotch Eggs | Egg Muffins | Almond Bread | Green Beans with Bacon | Egg Loaf |
| LUNCH  | Barbecue Pulled Pork | Perfect Italian Meatballs | Crispy Pork Carnitas | Chicken Pho | Honey Turkey Breast | Easy Lobster Bisque | Dan Dan Style Chicken |
| DINNER | Chunky Clam Chowder | Tom Kha Gai | Kale & Sausage Soup | Key Lime Pie | Lemon Custard | Crème Brulee | Collard Greens |

## WEEK 4

|       | SUN | MON | TUE | WED | THUR | FRI | SAT |
|---|---|---|---|---|---|---|---|
| B/FAST | Egg Cups | Green Beans with Bacon | Baba Ghanoush | Omelet with Chives | Tomato Frittata | Coconut Yogurt | Cauliflower Mac & Cheese |
| LUNCH | Paprika Chicken | Easy Lobster Bisque | Sesame Ginger Chicken | Spicy Turkey Cubes | Perfect Italian Meatball | Crispy Pork Carnitas | Taco Meat |
| DINNER | Tom Kha Gal | White Chicken Chili | Three Meat Chili | Chunky Clam Chowder | Chocolate Mousse | Cheese Cake | Key Lime Pie |

## WEEK 5

|       | SUN | MON | TUE | WED | THUR | FRI | SAT |
|---|---|---|---|---|---|---|---|
| B/FAST | Palak Paneer | Egg Muffins | Cauliflower Mac & Cheese | Egg Cups | Baba Ghanoush | Avocado Eggs Benedict | Almond Bread |
| LUNCH | Chicken Tikka Masala | Easy Lobster Bisque | Butter Chicken | Shrimp Scampi | Taco Meat | Crispy Pork Carnitas | Whole Chicken |
| DINNER | Lemon Custard | Key Lime Pie | Cheesecake | Crème Brulee | Three Meat Chili | Kale & Sausage Soup | Cauliflower Puree |

## WEEK 6

|       | SUN | MON | TUE | WED | THUR | FRI | SAT |
|---|---|---|---|---|---|---|---|
| B/FAST | Egg Cups | Shakshuka | Coconut Yogurt | Tomato Frittata | Tomato Frittata | Avocado Eggs Benedict | Almond Bread |
| LUNCH | Chicken Shawarma | Chicken Pho | Shrimp Scampi | Easy Lobster Bisque | Pork Belly | Chicken Korma | Taco Meat |
| DINNER | Cheese Cake | Lemon Custard | Collard Greens | Beef Stew | Lemon Garlic Broccoli | Chunky Clam Chowder | Sweet & Sour Cabbage |

## WEEK 7

|        | SUN | MON | TUE | WED | THUR | FRI | SAT |
|--------|-----|-----|-----|-----|------|-----|-----|
| B/FAST | Scotch Eggs | Shakshuka | Egg Cups | Egg Muffins | Tomato Frittata | Avocado Eggs Benedict | Almond Bread |
| LUNCH  | Chicken Shawarma | Chicken Pho | Honey Turkey Breast | Easy Lobster Bisque | Pork Belly | Mole Chicken | Taco Meat |
| DINNER | Cheese Cake | Lemon Custard | Chocolate Mousse | Beef Stew | Tom Kha Gai | Chunky Clam Chowder | Collard Greens |

## WEEK 8

|        | SUN | MON | TUE | WED | THUR | FRI | SAT |
|--------|-----|-----|-----|-----|------|-----|-----|
| B/FAST | Egg Cups | Green Beans with Bacon | Baba Ghanoush | Omelet with Chives | Tomato Frittata | Coconut Yogurt | Cauliflower Mac & Cheese |
| LUNCH  | Paprika Chicken | Easy Lobster Bisque | Sesame Ginger Chicken | Spicy Turkey Cubes | Perfect Italian Meatball | Crispy Pork Carnitas | Taco Meat |
| DINNER | Tom Kha Gal | White Chicken Chili | Three Meat Chili | Chunky Clam Chowder | Chocolate Mousse | Cheese Cake | Key Lime Pie |

## WEEK 9

|        | SUN | MON | TUE | WED | THUR | FRI | SAT |
|--------|-----|-----|-----|-----|------|-----|-----|
| B/FAST | Omelet with Chives | Palak Paneer | Egg Loaf | Baba Ghanoush | Tomato Frittata | Poblano and Cheese Frittata | Coconut Yogurt |
| LUNCH  | Lobster Tail | Garlic Chicken Pieces | Keto Chicken Thigh | Taco Meat | Barbacoa Beef | Hawaiian Pork | Philly Cheese Steak |
| DINNER | Tom Kha Gai | White Chicken Chili | No-Noodle Chicken Soup | Crème Brulee | Chocolate Mousse | Key Lime Pie | Marbled Pumpkin Cheesecake |

## WEEK 10

|        | SUN | MON | TUE | WED | THUR | FRI | SAT |
|--------|-----|-----|-----|-----|------|-----|-----|
| B/FAST | Shakashuka | Baba Ghanoush | Scotch Eggs | Egg Muffins | Almond Bread | Green Beans with Bacon | Egg Loaf |
| LUNCH  | Barbecue Pulled Pork | Perfect Italian Meatballs | Crispy Pork Carnitas | Chicken Pho | Honey Turkey Breast | Easy Lobster Bisque | Dan Dan Style Chicken |
| DINNER | Chunky Clam Chowder | Tom Kha Gai | Kale & Sausage Soup | Key Lime Pie | Lemon Custard | Crème Brulee | Collard Greens |

## WEEK 11

|        | SUN | MON | TUE | WED | THUR | FRI | SAT |
|--------|-----|-----|-----|-----|------|-----|-----|
| B/FAST | Egg Cups | Shakshuka | Coconut Yogurt | Tomato Frittata | Tomato Frittata | Avocado Eggs Benedict | Almond Bread |
| LUNCH  | Chicken Shawarma | Chicken Pho | Shrimp Scampi | Easy Lobster Bisque | Pork Belly | Chicken Korma | Taco Meat |
| DINNER | Cheese Cake | Lemon Custard | Collard Greens | Beef Stew | Lemon Garlic Broccoli | Chunky Clam Chowder | Sweet & Sour Cabbage |

## WEEK 12

|  | SUN | MON | TUE | WED | THUR | FRI | SAT |
|---|---|---|---|---|---|---|---|
| **B/FAST** | Palak Paneer | Egg Muffins | Cauliflower Mac & Cheese | Egg Cups | Baba Ghanoush | Avocado Eggs Benedict | Almond Bread |
| **LUNCH** | Chicken Tikka Masala | Easy Lobster Bisque | Butter Chicken | Shrimp Scampi | Taco Meat | Crispy Pork Carnitas | Whole Chicken |
| **DINNER** | Lemon Custard | Key Lime Pie | Cheesecake | Crème Brulee | Three Meat Chili | Kale & Sausage Soup | Cauliflower Puree |